Praise for *Reputation Matters*

"Amazing resource for those who wish to keep their finger on the pulse of not only today's key marketing issues, but those forecasted to plague us in the future. Alan is the ultimate communicator, both in branding and teaching, and we are so fortunate to benefit from his experience."

– Brenda Pritchard, Partner, Advertising, Marketing and Regulatory Affairs Practice at Gowling WLG and Canada's Marketing Hall of Legends inductee

"This is a most complete treatment of reputation management. Unlike others who take a one size fits all approach, Alan explicitly recognizes the different kinds of threats to reputation, the resultant need for a multidisciplinary toolbox and a diverse set of metrics including financial impact. He makes a strong case for responsibility to sit at the highest levels of management and provides mechanisms for weaving it into every aspect of the organization's operation. Whether you are in brand management, investor relations, supply chain or Human Resources, Alan provides a clear manifesto on how leaders build and preserve a rock solid reputation."

– Ken Wong, Distinguished Professor of Marketing and Business Strategy, Queen's University and Canada's Marketing Hall of Legends Inductee

"Alan Middleton has a keen understanding of brands and the value-based culture that are necessary to develop great people and products."

– Les Mandelbaum, President, UMBRA, and Canada's Marketing Hall of Legends Inductee

REPUTATION MATTERS

Why Branding & PR
is not Enough

REPUTATION MATTERS

Why Branding & PR is Not Enough

Alan C. Middleton PhD

CONTENTS

PREFACE

"Regard your good name as the richest jewel you can possibly be possessed of—for credit it is like fire: when once you have kindled it you may easily preserve it, but if you once extinguish it, you will find it an arduous task to rekindle it again. The way to gain a good reputation is to endeavour to be what you desire to appear."

– Socrates, 469–399 BC, Philosopher, Athens, Greece

In putting together this third book in the American Marketing Association Toronto (AMA Toronto) "Empowering Leadership Potential" series, I have been struck by the scale of this challenge in the business, government, not-for-profit, and academic communities. It is a journey. There is much bad practice that needs resolving, but there also have been positive changes. This book is an attempt to define what areas need focus and attention in marketing and other cross-silo organizational activities.

As the discipline of marketing evolves, so has the work of AMA Toronto. With the explosion of social media activity over the past 20 years or so, comments both factual and spurious about organizations and brands have grown. Marketing has always been concerned with the reputation of its organizations. Traditionally, this has been focused around its externally focused marketing communications activities (advertising, promotion, public relations, and social media) and brand building. More recently, concerns about organizational behaviour and the importance of clear internal and external policies and communication have become a key responsibility of marketing personnel. As such, internal as well as external audiences need to be addressed. In addition, the organization's values need to be defined as part of its vison and mission, and its policies and practices reviewed as an integral part of its activities. It is not just the customer brand communication but the reputation of the organization in total that now matters.

AMA Toronto is an award winning chapter of the American Marketing Association (AMA), headquartered in Chicago. With its 20,000 members, 70 professional chapters, and 250 collegiate chapters, AMA is the leading academic and operational community based marketing association on the globa stage. AMA Toronto, throughout its many activities, including awards like "Canada's Marketing Hall of Legends "and "Marketer on the Rise," events like the annual CMO and agency panels and the Legendary Leadership series, mentorship through 13 years of the coveted "Mentor Exchange" program and the "Career Accelerator" program, leadership development programs like "Executive Coaching", and publications like these books, is a leading marketing not-for-profit service organization contributing to the professional community in Canada. In 2021, AMA Toronto earned the "Silver Chapter" award in the global AMA organization, and in 2022 it earned five AMA Excellence Awards.

Once again, I am grateful for the support of AMA Toronto and its Board, Advisory Council and volunteers, and particularly Barbara Boyd, the AMA president, and Miglena Nikolova and Craig Lund for their input, support, and friendship.

Alan Middleton
May 2023

INTRODUCTION

"It takes 20 years to build a reputation and five minutes to ruin it. If you think about that you'll do things differently."

– Warren Buffett, American financial entrepreneur. Chair, CEO Berkshire Hathaway

These days it is hard to view or listen to any media, be it traditional or social, and not be exposed to negative stories about business, trade unions, not-for-profits, associations, and governments. There are so many that as a manager in these organizations one may be tempted to regard them as unimportant or that they will go away and there will be no significant harm to the organization. While rare and minor issues may not have huge impacts on an organization's reputation and activities in the short term, failing to pay attention and develop policies and practices that reduce vulnerability is just poor management practice.

This book will review research cases and suggest policies and practices. Often referred to as ethics and compliance issues, these have too often been left to legal and compliance groups in organizations. These issues impact the overall reputation of the organization and need to be addressed at all levels across the whole organization. All levels in all organizations contribute to best practices that can lead to a strong positive reputation and positive stakeholder views that benefit the organization financially and operationally.

So, what is reputation? Dictionary.com defines it as "The estimation in which a person or thing is held, especially by the community or public generally."

Who are the "community and public" in this case? They are stakeholders like customers, potential customers, and investors. They are voters and taxpayers. They are regulatory and legislative personnel. For all organizations they are also, most importantly, the staff, suppliers, and partners of the organization who are too often overlooked or ignored.

As we will see in this book, two increasingly important issues in reputation management are ethics and compliance. Dictionary.com defines these as follows:

Ethics: "a system of moral principles."

Compliance: "the act of conforming or yielding as with orders or laws. Usually used in reference to written rules and regulations."

Reviews of research, literature, and practice indicates that this topic of organization reputation management has been addressed by three types of initiative:

Legal, Ethics, and Compliance

Often motivated by anti-bribery legislation such as the US Foreign Corrupt Practices Act (FCPA) of 1997, a Canadian version The Corruption of Foreign Public Officials Act (CFPOA) of 1998, and the U.K. equivalent Bribery Act of 2010, this led legal departments into broader ethics and compliance activities. Additionally other legislation has included elements of prescribed financial and operational practice.

Recently in the US, a number of societies focusing on these areas have been increasingly active. Examples include:

- ECI (Ethics & Compliance Initiative) founded in 1922 and headquartered in Vienna, Virginia, with global membership, it "empowers organizations to build and sustain High-Quality Ethics & Compliance Programs (HQPs)." Its primary activities are in research and certificated training programs and in awards to recognise individual and organization contribution.

- SCCE (Society of Corporate Compliance & Ethics) founded in 2004 and incorporated in 2011, headquartered in Minneapolis, Minnesota, "Exists to champion ethical practices and compliance standards and to provide necessary resources for ethics and compliance professionals and others who share these principles." They also offer lobbying, training and events.

- Trace International (Trade Reporting and Compliance Engine) founded in 1996, headquartered in Annapolis, Maryland, with global membership, representatives in Canada, India, Mexico, and the Philippines, whose mission is: "A globally recognised non-profit business association dedicated to anti-bribery, compliance and good governance."

Many have been setting standards and certification. Ethisphere through its "The Sphere" survey publishes a yearly list of the "World's Most Ethical Companies": In 2023 there were 135 companies from 19 countries. It is based on their analysis of five areas: Governance; Leadership and Reputation; Culture of Ethics; Ethics and Compliance Program and Environmental Social Impact.

These moves and others have been accelerated by a number of well-publicised corporate bad behaviours. These have included Volkswagen in the US in 2015 when the Environmental Protection Agency found the company had falsified emission data. In 2015 Valeant Pharmaceuticals was found to have falsified demand for its pharmaceuticals and had substantially raised prices. Facebook in 2018 was discovered to have released client data to Global Sciences Research without permission of its clients. In Canada, in 2022 alone, Tim Hortons was fined in a legal action for violating privacy laws in its customer data use; BCE/Bell Media showed poor management practice in age and gender discrimination in its primary CTV channel; and Hockey Canada Board and management were recalcitrant in accepting appropriate social standards in its public denial of a history of sexual harassment in its games, and secret payouts to victims.

Branding

The whole notion of marketing work around branding is to achieve the highest positive reputation amongst its target group of customers so that consumers in B2C and organizations engaged in a B2B trial have repeat purchase at rates higher than competitors. In my books and lectures on branding I have defined a brand as follows: "To its target group of customers and their influencers, a promise of benefits consistently delivered with the highest level of satisfaction versus direct and indirect competitors."

All too often though, practitioners and commentators have ignored the critically important group that deliver the benefits and, in a largely service economy, are an essential part of the benefits: the staff of the brand. I learned this very early on in my practitioner career from a client who was then president of Toyota Canada, Suzuki-san, who said to me:

"Staff [at the company and its dealers] and customers are two sides of the same coin."

The reputation of a brand is not just delivered in its product/service design, pricing, place (channels of distribution), and promotion (marketing communication) but most importantly its people and their ethical and compliant behaviour. The point is that all employees—not just senior management—need to be briefed, trained, and take actions to deliver ethical and compliant behaviour to build and protect the overall reputation of the brand. Too often brand policies and practices have ignored this!

The other emerging issue in branding is that for more and more organizations the corporate name is the primary brand. This is true of most automotive, energy, financial services, IT, retail, telecommunications organizations. It is increasingly also a focus in other sectors like the consumer health and pharmaceutical and the packaged goods industry that have developed individual product brands. Many are now promoting the overall corporate brand as well. Procter and Gamble and Unilever amongst others are doing this. This increasing focus on the corporate brand means its reputation in all aspects of its activity is a key issue.

Public Relations

Dictionary.com defines public relations as: "The actions of a corporation, store, government, individual, etc., in promoting goodwill between itself and the public, the community, employees, customers, etc."

In reviewing the literature around reputation, the largest amount was from the public relations viewpoint consisting of both how to promote an organization's reputation positively to key target groups (under the "crisis management" heading) and how to manage when negatives emerged.

Both are important elements in reputation management but not sufficient. Too often the role of public relations is to "accentuate the positive, eliminate the negative" (Johnny Mercer, 1945, American lyricist and singer). While this is not wrong, in the contemporary world of reputation management it is not adequate. Public relations activity now needs to be involved with other senior management, owners, staff, suppliers, and partners in establishing clear vision, values, and practices so that the reputation of the organization is based on social equity and positive ethical practices and not just reactions to problems caused from its own operations and practices.

As the remainder of this book will go on to argue, the strategic hierarchy so long taught in business schools needs to pay greater attention to the "Values" category that has for too long not received sufficiently serious attention by people at the most senior levels of organizations.

Reputation Management Tool: The Strategy Hierarchy Path to Reputation Management

Values

Vision/Mission

- What you want to accomplish that provides a benefit to a set of customers in a way that delivers value to all stakeholders (shareholders, staff, suppliers, community)

Values

- What values you wish to bring to society and your organization: ethical views and behaviour.

Goals

- What measurable achievements you want to attain to satisfy customers and stakeholders.

Strategy

- How you will attain those goals with the values you ascribe to: scope, scale, speed, cost/finance, marketing, brand, risk assessment

Resources, Culture and Structure

- The key enablers of the strategy.

Tactics

- How you will specifically deliver components of the strategy: new products and services, acquire, merge, alliances, reorganize etc.

Implementation

- What you will do, when, by whom, with what resources and how you will measure achievement and then respond.

Cases and Viewpoints: The Johnson & Johnson Credo

A well-regarded statement of vision and mission that includes its values is Johnson & Johnson: an almost US$100 billion pharmaceutical, medical technology. and consumer healthcare company headquartered in New Jersey, USA.

Our Credo

We believe our first responsibility is to the patients, doctors and nurses, to mothers and fathers, and all others who use our products and services. In meeting their needs everything we do must be of high quality. We must constantly strive to provide value, reduce our costs, and maintain reasonable prices. Customers' orders must be serviced promptly and accurately. Our business partners must have an opportunity to make a fair profit.

We are responsible to our employees who work with us throughout the world. We must provide an inclusive work environment where each person must be considered as an individual. We must respect their diversity and dignity and recognize their merit. They must have a sense of security, fulfillment, and purpose in their jobs. Compensation must be fair and adequate and working conditions clean, orderly, and safe. We must support the health and well-being of our employees and help them fulfill their family and other personal responsibilities. Employees must feel free to make suggestions and complaints. There must be equal opportunity for employment, development and advancement for those qualified. We must provide highly capable leaders and their actions must be just and ethical.

We are responsible to the communities in which we live and work and to the world community as well. We must help people be healthier by supporting better access and care in more places around the world. We must be good citizens: to support good works and charities, better health and education, and bear our fair share of taxes. We must maintain in good order the property we are privileged to use, protecting the environment and natural resources.

Our final responsibility is to our stockholders. Business must make a sound profit. We must experiment with new ideas. Research must be carried on, innovative programs developed, investments made for the future, and mistakes paid for. New equipment must be purchased, new facilities provided, and new products launched. Reserves must be created to provide for adverse times. When we operate according to these principles, the stockholders should realize a fair return.

CHAPTER 1
REPUTATION ISSUES: OVERVIEW

"Character is like a tree and reputation is like its shadow. The shadow is what we think of it, the tree is the real thing."

– Abraham Lincoln, 1809–1865, American President 1861–1865 and statesman

"Learn from the mistakes of others. You can't live long enough to make them all yourself."

– Eleanor Roosevelt, 1884–1962, American former First Lady 1933–1945

Research and review of practices indicate five major areas that contribute to negative reputational impact:

1. Poor, misleading, or illegal financial management.

2. Data misuse or data hacking.

3. Viral customer complaints for poor product quality, service, misleading pricing or treatment.

4. A toxic organizational culture and/or employment/remuneration bias.

5. Lack of clarity, communication, understanding or training in ethical and compliance behaviour by all levels of staff.

Any organization's reputation policy needs to address all five of these and have them applied at all levels in the organization as well as to partners and suppliers. Issues that harm reputation and, with it, the regard of customers, staff, investors, government and partners has an impact on market demand, earnings, share price, and investor confidence.

Historically, negative impacts can be caused by both major issues and/or continued more minor negatives. The organization has two clear responsibilities to protect its reputation:

1. As far as possible develop both a policy of ethical behaviours and compliance, and ensure it is well communicated, understood, and acted on by all staff levels;

2. Ensure false or misleading information is challenged with all stakeholders.

So, what is the cost?

Some argue, and continue to do so, that the cost of full application of such a policy is too relative to the financial harm that is caused. This is short-sighted from two perspectives:

- The harm is sometimes major and measurable as with a number of well publicized cases. However, frequent smaller transgressions may not be as measurable in the short term, but the reputation amongst some stakeholders suffers "death by a thousand cuts" ("lingchi" an old Chinese form of execution). Customer and potential customer brand choice may be weakened, price/value expectations lowered, investor attraction reduced, and government legislative attention activated.

- The second harm is that it may offset other policies to help build a healthy, positive, ethical organization culture. A culture that attracts and retains the best people. A culture that develops superior products and services. A culture that customers and suppliers want to do business with.

The point is that in the contemporary environment of media and social media coverage reputation management is a major strategic issue to be addressed. More and more organizations are recognizing this and appointing senior executives to develop policies and practices that cover the five areas outlined. It is a major task, as it requires analysis, policy development, communication, training and constant reinforcement across organization silos.

Cases and Viewpoints #1.1: Interview with Emmanuel Lulin of L'Oréal

"At L'Oréal, our six values are at the heart of everything. Passion, Innovation, Entrepreneurial Spirit, Open-mindedness, Quest for Excellence and Responsibility are our guidelines."

Emmanuel Lulin, former Senior VP and Chief Ethics Officer L'Oréal. Senior VP 1999–2021; previously since 1989 General Counsel. L'Oréal S.A., headquartered in Paris, France, is a Euro 35 billion personal care and cosmetics company. It is the world's largest cosmetic company.

Prior to L'Oréal Lulin worked for law firm Debevoise & Plimpton in France and had earned degrees from University of Chicago and in France. At age 18 he was involved with activists Serge and Beate Klarsfeld in tracking down Nazis.

He was the first non-American to receive the prestigious Carol R. Marshall Award from the Ethics & Compliance Initiative in 2015 and was the first individual recognized by the United Nations as a UN Global Compact SDG Pioneer for Advancing Business Ethics in 2018. He then received a Lifetime Achievement in Compliance honor at Compliance Week's 2021 Excellence in Compliance Awards.

Emmanuel's passion for justice and ethical behaviour has been a theme throughout his life and career. A personal experience of being accused of doing something he didn't do at a very young age, and then the post-war tendency for European governments to avoid dealing with some of the issues of the 1930s and 1940s led him towards his life's journey:

"From early in my life I had an interest in fairness and justice and at the age of 15 met Serge and Beate Klarsfeld. They encouraged me to work with them which I was very glad to do so to show that my generation shared understanding and solidarity with my parent's generation and show that we were not forgetting."

Always interested in law, his studies and work took him into the legal profession both in France and the US. He moved from corporate and tax into labour practice. Based on legislative changes at this time in the

US, compliance issues were emerging as an area of attention. Back in France employed by L'Oréal this background and his personal interest led to his work on the first L'Oréal Charter of Ethics. Work had already started but his mission was to not only have an important code but to make it practical: "What was lacking from the US focus on compliance was an ethics approach based on values and sincerity."

This focus on building values based on sincere commitment rather than just compliance to law is central to how Emmanuel views both the topic and the implementation of standards and behaviour: the need to build an ethical organization culture:

"I am talking about creating an asset that is not measured enough, and that is trust. Trust is a currency of ethics. The more ethical you are and behave, the more you create trust. All organizations need the trust of employees, colleagues, Board, investors, customers, suppliers, the public. It is not just about trust in the short term. Here by a 'big lie' you can create short term trust. The issue is to create trust over time and this must be measured by more than compliance. If you don't have trust, your business is in bad shape."

Recognizing that ethics are in part impacted by region, religion, history and culture, ethical standards need to represent what practices the organization views as important, what Emmanuel calls *"To take a stand. What will help the organization and its people make a decision when there is a choice. For instance, at L'Oréal we thought that integrity, courage, transparency were key values."*

The key to take a stand is to have discussion around the values and ethics, their implementation and the trade-offs often involved. This can only be accomplished by connecting "on the ground" in the operations with the staff, customers and community involved in their local environment. As Emmanuel says, this "bottom up" approach is essential for building an effective ethical culture:

"Building a mission around ethics it is essential to get to know the people and the issues in their work lives. So, I visited the factories, the distribution centres, the marketing teams, all the functions, and talked to everyone top to bottom. Open discussions, in the absence of management when needed. To know the reality on the ground is absolutely key. You can't do this from headquarters and the ivory tower."

Many times, this was not just about meetings and questions and answers but viewing facilities, like the washrooms/toilets for working staff, to understand their physical and mental environment. Staff surveys and questionnaires have their role, but are not adequate. This is especially true with international organizations where local cultural practices differ. This local input is, in his view, also critical in applying the standards and indeed, their measurement.

So how to measure? As Emmanuel says, if you only have one question, do it privately and with guarantee of anonymity:

"Do you feel free to speak up without fear of reprisals?"

As Emmanuel says it is good practice for both ethical but also strategic and operational decisions:

"We make better decisions when we feel free to speak up. We can share flaws and concerns and discuss them."

Another question to ask would be: What are the values and the code of ethics of the organization? And if not readily memorable, how easy is it for the employee/customer/public to access them?

Too often, even when there is a well-developed code and statements, these are not actively promoted and people trained in their implementation at an operational level. Good ethical decisions need to be disseminated widely.

In reviewing the ethical issues discussed in this book—misleading financial information, data mismanagement, toxic workplaces, poor customer service and pricing and lack of clear policies, practices and communications in ethical behaviour—Emmanuel sees transparency as a key foundational solution. Transparency:

- By organizations publishing codes of ethics and their application, and what they have done to mitigate/explain bad practices;

- By industry and professional associations to publish reports and surveys on the ethical activities of their members and themselves;

- Universities and especially business, law, and engineering faculties in not only having compulsory ethics courses, but revealing where their graduates are in senior management levels linked with good or poor ethical practices.

While not yet extensive enough, Emmanuel feels that more senior executives in both private and public organizations are taking the issues of ethical behaviours seriously. Transparency International and other research organizations are producing data relating to both perception and cases. (In the 2022 Corruption Perception Index the Scandinavian countries along with New Zealand and Singapore were rated as the least corrupt. Canada ranked #14; USA ranked #24 out of 180 countries ranked.)

In addition, changes in government policy are focusing on this topic. An example is the December 2019 appointment of Vera Jourov as European Commissioner for Values and Transparency. This organization reviews public information and data for its opaqueness, transparency, and clarity.

As the chapters in this book discuss, part of the reason for the growing interest in organizational ethical behaviour is due to reputational risk from exposure in social media. It is also a dawning recognition that some of the principles Emmanuel talks about lead to better governance and strategic and operational decision making:

"A better ethical culture is a key driver for long term success."

The key in Emmanuel's view is the character and responsibility of the chief ethics officer, working with the support of the Board and the CEO/COO in the private sector, or the minister and president/prime minister and chief administrative officer in the public sector. In order to perform the role well, key elements include access to information and data on a regular basis and the fortitude to resist opposition from more compliance-only perspectives. One "test" of the organization's commitment that Emmanuel suggests is whether a call or text from the public to the organization head office to request a connection to the chief ethics officer is fulfilled. Another is to review the structure of senior management compensation and the rewards and penalties for achieving or missing financial only targets versus the other areas of organizational health.

Training is another area for focus. Emmanuel believes training in ethics should be part of all academic, professional, and practitioner training programs, not just accounting (like the CPA work described in Chapter 2.1) and law but also manufacturing, R&D, HR, sales, marketing and public relations, and so on. This training and education need to be continuous.

Changes in both legislation but also and more importantly in ethical standards need to be tracked, and organizational responses updated. Issues like conflict of interest get ever more complicated (like the We charity scandal of 2020). Relationship issues constantly emerge (like the Toronto Mayor resignation of February 2023). Changes in global supply chains (like China and Russia sourcing in 2022/2023). Changes in policies relating to ESG (Environment, Social Governance) are all ongoing (for instance, environmental issues like pollution as well as the emerging issue of use of water). In Emmanuel's view fundamental business issues continue to present the greatest opportunity for ethical improvement:

"Which product to sell. What are the ingredients. What is the sourcing of the products. How the products are marketed. Who we send the products to. What are the claims. What is it that we don't say about the product! Business related issues, and very often these are ignored."

Final Tips from Emmanuel Lulin

- "Ethics is about agreeing and adhering to values: for compliance you obey and for ethics you agree. The approach is different: values change, law changes less."

- Key question for staff: "Do you feel able to speak up without fear of reprisal?"

- It is about justice in your organization.

- Sharing and gaining of positive and negative information is key to the role of ethics application.

- Organizations need ethical policies and practices to be clear about what is expected from the individual. How to handle ambiguity. How does my direct boss behave and how do they treat employees/ suppliers/customers?

- Work bottom-up in preparing policies and procedures, not top down. But when ready, align the Code of Ethics to Board and senior management policy and remuneration.

Red Flags from Emmanuel Lulin

Here are some classic excuses for ignoring ethical policies and practices:

- Let's just do it once.

- No one will ever know.

- Everyone does it.

- It's just part of the culture here.

- We can cover it in a memo.

- I can't find an explicit policy against it.

How to resist:

- Okay, let's just tell everyone what we are doing.

Interview in person with Emmanuel Lulin, Toronto, February 20 and 21, 2023.

Cases and Viewpoints #1.2: Reputation Management at Save the Children Canada

Save the Children Canada is one of 30 members of Save the Children International, which works in over 100 countries worldwide. Founded in 1919 in the UK, the Canadian organization was founded in 1921 and follows its mission: "….to advance children's rights around the world. We do whatever it takes every day and in times of crisis—to give children a healthy start in life, the opportunity to learn, and protection from harm. We strive to ensure children's unique needs are met and their voices are heard—transforming their lives and the future we share. Because we believe every girl and boy has the right to survive and thrive."

Interview with Danny Glenwright, President and CEO, and Jessica Bryant, Head of Communications, Media and PR. Danny's background experience is in journalism and not-for-profits around the world. Jessica was previously at Save the Children International in the UK.

Save the Children works across issues of survival: learning, gender equity, protection, emergencies like the climate crisis, the hunger crisis, earthquakes in Turkey and Syria, and conflicts in the Ukraine and Yemen. Additionally, in Canada it operates the National Reconciliation Program, a national Indigenous child rights program. As part of the organization's commitment to reconciliation, it operates as an additional resource for Indigenous communities and organizations supporting community-led programming, services and initiatives.

Working with stakeholders like Global Affairs Canada and other partners and donors, the new strategic plan calls for greater engagement of local organizations to lead and implement activities. The purpose is to gain greater engagement and local knowledge and application. As Danny says:

"We are de-colonizing our sectors and focusing on really living our values as an organization. We see our future as doing less of telling our partners what to do and much more fundraising and working with them to implement programs as they see the need. This is easier to do with our

local partners in Canada, but we are also influencing the global federation to move in this direction."

Jessica confirms that this de-colonization policy is setting the direction for brand and reputation building with media and with donors.

"We are putting in a lot of effort to grow the brand in Canada. Because of the direct nature of social media activity, a lot of the work is handling reputational issues—both internal and sometimes external—in the sector we are in. For example, QAnon used "Save the Children" in their hashtag which we had to manage and inform the public that this was not related to our organization."

Like many organizations faced with endless social media comments—both good and bad—about their activities, a judgment has to be made which require a response. As Jessica says:

"What should we do about comments on our social media posts? Which do we respond to? How do we respond? How do we manage our messages when we are an active part of community engagement? The key priority is how to build trust. We can put all the right things in the world in place to get across that we act with integrity, are accountable, and transparent, but we are still going to be subject to erroneous information."

Another reputational issue that impacted the sector was the Oxfam scandal during 2018 in the UK regarding sexual exploitation in Haiti and the subsequent flawed investigation. Though Save the Children had no involvement with it, they still had to handle the stories. In Canada they handled it in an open manner and addressed it head on it rather than ignoring it. Save the Children is committed to creating a culture where sexual abuse, assault, harassment, or misconduct in any form is rooted out. They know that no organization is immune to abuses of power, but they do what it takes to inoculate their own culture against it.

"We put in a lot more policies and process about treatment of staff and our partners."

In situations where there are legitimate issues involving Save the Children, they take the view to own the issue, address it and be accountable. Danny comments,

"It is not just about having policies and signing documents. It needs a sustainable, inbred approach. We have discussions on our team about these issues and what to do about them: we need to communicate that we take these issues seriously."

A lot of work has been done on safeguarding issues because of issues coming up in the sector involving child and gender protection and so on. In this, and other issues, Danny comments,

"It is not just ticking a check box and saying the training is done, it needs constant attention and feedback mechanisms: what it means in a country office in rural Nigeria, not just the head office! It needs an organization-wide values approach. You make sure the systems and procedures are all clear when you join and throughout your engagement with us. Make sure that when they err, there are consequences."

Key to understanding the not-for-profit sector's role, according to Danny, is to recognize its limitations. It will never fix all the problems it deals with but can help. Part of that help is in the way it operates and this is, in part, transferring more responsibility closer to the area, geographically or philosophically, of the partner operation. This shift needs real commitment to living the values through a motivating code of ethics and its constant updating and reinforcement based on lived experiences.

As Jessica comments,

"We don't only get questions about where the money goes and how is it spent, but much broader questions about the ethics of our operation and its partner activities. This is all charged up by social media. There is a lot more public discussion and debate about these things and we are rightly held accountable for how we respond and act."

Fund raising at Save the Children Canada is nowadays much more strategic and targeted so understanding of how the brand is seen is a critical part of the process. This is especially true of situations where fund raising for crises or emergencies like the war in Ukraine must not hinder fund raising in areas needing ongoing contribution. Save the Children does have The Children's Emergency Fund, which is a restricted pool of money that enables rapid response to crises. They equally have funds that are focused on longer term children's needs.

Often, in times of crisis and as a response to them, aid agencies come together under the umbrella of the Humanitarian Coalition to coordinate appeals: it includes twelve organizations like Care Canada, Plan Canada, Save the Children Canada, and World Vision Canada.

The key in ethical application in reputation management for Save the Children Canada is to have clear codes of practice and policies, and reinforcing them at all levels and especially in local partner markets. There is also the need for all parties involved to realize that these are all communication issues as well and to involve the relevant people. There are social media and other policies as a guideline, but the key is to constantly review and engage everyone. As Jessica sees it, to support and build the overall brand reputation in communication: "Be on top of social issues, recognize their impact both on staff and externally, and in our communication: Be simple. Be powerful. Be consistent."

Interview March 21, 2023.

CHAPTER 2
REPUTATION ISSUES: POOR, MISLEADING OR ILLEGAL FINANCIAL MANAGEMENT

"A single lie destroys a whole reputation of integrity."

– Baltasar Gracian, 1601–1658, Spanish writer and philosopher.

Financial standards are seemingly well regulated via legislation and through institutions like the International Financial Reporting Standards (IFRS). In Canada these include the provincial accounting regulations of the Chartered Professional Accountants (CPA), the Canadian Public Accountability Board (CPAB), and the Accounting Standards Board (AcSB). In the US the Financial Accounting Standards Board (FASP) and its Accounting Standards Certification (ASC) use Generally Accepted Accounting Principles (GAAP) analysis. In addition, the federal Consumer Financial Protection Bureau provides legislation for compliance. The European Union (EU) adopted IFRS standards in 2002. As such, while well regulated in most countries globally, differences and other behaviours have resulted in subtle and not so subtle examples of misleading financial data or illegal financial activities.

Sadly, the period since the 1990s has seen constant examples of deliberate misconduct as well as ethically questionable practices: E.F. Hutton (now defunct brokerage firm); Drexel Burnham Lambert (Michael Milken's firm); Salomon Brothers; Merrill Lynch and its misinformation to its Orange County client; Bankers Trust and its misinformation to its P&G client; unauthorized trading in Barings Bank in Singapore; New York State lawsuits against a number of mutual fund operations; Enron (see case at the end of this chapter); World Com; the financial crisis of 2007–2009 caused by unsuitable loans in the mortgage sector; the collapse of MF Global and the Knight Capital Group; Wells Fargo; Luckin Coffee; Wirecard in Germany; JP Morgan through its acquisition of Frank; and most recently FTX and its crypto fund scheme.

Outside of compliance issues and breaches, how should ethical issues be viewed? John Boatright in his book provides a useful definition: "Ethics in finance consists of moral norms that apply to financial activity broadly conceived. Moral norms in this context may be understood as prescribed guides for behavior or conduct about what is right or wrong or about what ought to be done using such concepts as duty or obligation, rights and fairness or justice."

Boatright suggests that the key elements of ethics can be expressed as six questions:

1. Welfare: Is anyone being harmed, and if so, can the harm be justified?

2. Duty: What is my duty or obligation in this situation?

3. Rights: Are anyone's rights being violated, and if so, can the violation be justified?

4. Justice: Is everyone being treated fairly or justly?

5. Honesty: Am I being entirely honest in my actions?

6. Dignity: Am I showing respect for all persons involved?

What are the causes of illegal or bad conduct happening with such frequency as described earlier? Analysts and commentators identify many reasons:

- Pressure and culture: A pressure to achieve financial objectives as the dominant criteria for financial and career progress. Others who act in this way are seen as succeeding more than others in the same organization or industry. Without strong senior management leadership to the contrary, this becomes the prevailing culture of the organization.

- Organizational factors: These include diffused responsibility across organization silos and where no one is charged with compliance or ethical responsibility. Also, there are instances of poor technology and systems. Perhaps most important is poor senior executive management in terms of ethical and compliant leadership and in establishing a healthy work culture.

- Innovation: Innovation often creates new situations so that legislation or ethical standards are non-existent or unclear. Also, innovation often causes shifts in risks and responsibilities that the organization has not considered. Additionally, the impacts of innovation are often unclear, so issues emerge that have not been considered. Sometimes the innovation gives the organization a leading competitive advantage that staff and management do not want to risk by investigating too closely.

Readers will note that despite the problems mentioned earlier many of these organizations are still in business, albeit with weakened reputations. The problems continue globally: In January 2023 the huge Brazilian retailer Americanas was found to have concealed billions of Reals in debt on its financial statements over a decade. Poor handling of financial matters does not automatically mean organization failure due to other strengths that the organization has developed. However, the evidence is strong that the organization's reputation suffers and along with other issues, reduces the value and effectiveness of it.

It is encouraging that organizations like the CPA take these issues seriously, as evidenced by their training and development activities such as one held at the end of 2022; my notes on this session follow.

Cases and Viewpoints #2.1: CPA Ontario.

"Ethics in Practice"

– CPA Ontario Seminar December 8, 2022.

The accounting profession is one of the professional groups now taking ethical behaviours as well as legal compliance as an important part of its practice. In late 2022 the Ontario CPA held a public seminar where its speakers emphasised ethical issues as important beyond just compliance. The following is a summary of the compelling points made by its speakers. Please note these are my comments and summary, not the actual presentations of the speakers.

CPA Speaker #1: Janet Gilles, Executive Vice-President Regulatory & Standards, CPA Ontario.

Ms. Gilles reviewed a recent history of the costs, both monetary and reputational, of ethics and compliance violations. In monetary terms, cases like Enron, BP, Wells Fargo, and more recently in Canada, Hockey Canada show financial impact but it also impacts HR: hiring and retaining top talent. In surveys 39% of staff say they will quit rather than engage in unethical behaviour. CPA Ontario recognizes the pressure of competition and goal achievement to succeed in business but believe that trust in financial ethical practices is at the heart of the profession and therefore the knowledge and training that CPA Ontario provides.

During the pandemic CPA Ontario and Brock University published a research study titled "Virtual Reality" on how business organizations can prepare students with virtual reality practice in real life ethical decision making. It helps focus not on what people think they might do, but how decisions get made in real world situations. This is a consistent focus throughout the speaker remarks that follow.

CPA Speaker #2: Morgan Hamel, President MH Partners, Calgary; Business Ethics Professional, Consultants on Reputation Management. Master degree in Applied & Professional Ethics, Utrecht University in the Netherlands; then CNOOC Calgary then consultancy.

"Becoming as Ethical as We Think We Are. Preventing Moral Injury in the post-2012 Era."

– Morgan Hamel

In a previously co-authored essay, Morgan indicates that "We are in a new era of stakeholder activism. Companies, Boards and senior individuals will be forced to speak out on a number of social issues and develop appropriate internal culture, policies and procedures." *The Economist*, in its "World Ahead 2023," edition agrees: "Companies will be increasingly expected to engage with sociopolitical issues, from abortion to racial justice."

Morgan Hamel focuses on the post 2012 era as in 2012 social media "likes," "sharers," and influencers became more important in forming information—both factual and false—about organizations.

Post-2012 pressure on organizations and its leaders comes from all forms of stakeholders: investors, staff, lobby groups, governments, and individuals. When not handled well, the information can have a significant impact on both business and reputation.

Additionally, according to Edelman surveys a majority of employees and potential employees look at these issues online when considering their employment status. Research from the UK indicates a rise in "workplace activism" in social media, and in some cases in other ways (e.g., lawsuits). The concept of "moral injury" has developed where workplace behaviour can contradict personal moral and ethical beliefs. This conflict, often disguised as "burnout," is forecast to have significant impact on efficiency and earnings.

Traditional policies and practices to manage ethical issues like having core value statements, codes of ethics, and limited staff communication continue to be important, but not adequate in the post-2012 era. Recent examples include:

- Disney: The now departed CEO, Bob Chapek, responded late to the "Don't Say Gay" bill in Florida despite employee pressure. Disney was found to have made political contributions to politicians who supported the bill that banned school instruction on sexual orientation and gender identity from kindergarten to Grade 3. Stock price fell 15% and the CEO was replaced.

- Old Navy: Its "size inclusivity" program for women's clothing ended up with supply problems in small and plus sizes and dissatisfied customers with sizes that didn't fit. Sales dropped 19% and the CEO, Nancy Green, left.

- Wells Fargo: The company expanded its employment diversity hiring program and set targets. In practice as they did not find enough to fill the targets. The company also set up fake interviews. On discovery, stock price fell and litigation is pending.

So how do organizations and their people make better ethical decisions? By understanding its complexity and giving training that is real world in confronting often opposing views or value systems. Additionally, by using "thought tools" to help people address ethical issues and what she terms "stakeholder polarization": contradictory views of different stakeholders. She used a wonderful 2021 UK commercial for Heineken titled "Worlds Apart" to dramatize the issue and thoughts for resolution.

One of the thought tools she suggests for engaging opposing views on challenging socio-economic/ethical issues is what she terms "Step Left. Step Right." We should try not to think of right or wrong but a spectrum of views. At each stage of the thinking or conversation we should determine how it might be possible to step slightly left to a more liberal view or step slightly right to a more conservative view, and invite the others in the conversation to do the same.

Another thought tool is for us to recognize our own blind spots: areas where we don't do what, in theory, we think we will do. This is the "want" versus "should" dilemma. We should (emotionally) do the right ethical thing, but due to circumstance, peer pressure, and/or perceived risk (reputational or physical) we use the rational part of our brain and do what we want (rationally) for our perceived benefit. Based on this behavioural research it has been found that managers who view themselves as "professional"—more focused on the "want"—are more likely to behave less ethically! In the fashion industry, for example, surveys show managers rate child labour as less serious than others and reality. How do we overcome this?

Another thought tool she suggests is the "self-interest snap." In our thinking and discussion on work issues, we should pause, recognize our "want" orientation, and create a mental "snap." Then reflect on/rethink the issue—and maybe apply "step left/step right" or at least think more about the decision and its consequences.

One example cited of the "want" versus "should" ethical dilemma for professionals was the Ernst & Young (EY) accounting scandal. Forty-nine EY professionals "obtained or circulated" answer keys to CPA license exams and hundreds of others lied about completing ongoing professional education courses.

The underlying problem with ethics is that we view ourselves as more ethical than we are and, especially as professionals, need to use some thought tools to better enable reflection and conversation. Unless we change behaviour, we risk increasing damage and distrust in both personal and organizational reputation.

CPA Speaker #3: Lisa Dorion; extensive experience in ethics, compliance and risk management and their strategic application including Chief Risk Officer Corporate Finance Institute. Board member of a variety of organizations in the private and public sector. Chartered accountant and Master of Studies in Law, Fordham University.

"Why Compliance Programs Fail"

As one commentator has said (Emmanuel Lulin ex-Executive VP Legal and Ethics L'Oréal globally) compliance policies are not a guarantee of ethical behaviour but they can help.

Compliance programs vary in their structure based on size of organization: less in small organizations (under 100 employees), more in medium ones (100–500 employees). Many large organizations these days have some elements of a compliance program. These can be defined in four ways:

1. Robust Compliance Program: code of conduct policies; conflict of interest policies; HR policies on diversity and inclusion, whistleblowing policies; training in, and frequent communication of, the application of these policies.

2. Partial Approach: code of conduct plus some compliance and HR policies.

3. Limited Approach: some compliance and HR policies.

4.   No developed or activated compliance program.

While the first two strategies can help, compliance does not guarantee ethical actions. Some recent examples of organizations with extensive compliance programs demonstrate this. Boeing, BP, and Wells Fargo have all had multiple ethical and compliance breaches publicized, and all are in highly regulated business environments.

Boeing: While being a sponsor of the Ethics & Compliance Initiative survey (!), the company was responsible for the 737 MAX aircraft breach of operational and ethical procedures. It used the MCAS flight control software that had proved unreliable. Two crashes occurred killing 346 people. Legal settlements cost it $21 billion and additional costs in lost business and so on are estimated at $65 billion. As well as lasting reputation loss.

BP: Its Deepwater Horizon oil spill in the Gulf of Mexico was a huge environmental disaster. One of the causes was using procedures that had already failed earlier in their Caspian Sea facility. Found guilty in 14 lawsuits, cost to BP is estimated at over $5 billion, and again reputation loss.

Wells Fargo: The company was found guilty of encouraging some 5,000 employees to create fraudulent accounts or falsify customer data in its attempt to increase cross-selling of its products. Cost to the company was over $3 billion and once again, reputation loss.

These companies may have been "too big to fail" but as Enron proved, not always and for small and medium size organizations not at all. An example would be the 2020 WE Charity scandal where the organization won a $912 million Canadian government contract for summer student programs, and had paid money to political figures in the government. WE Charity no longer exists.

Compliance policies are about policies and procedures designed to protect the organization but they are not *the* organizational culture. The task is to have ethical leadership, employees *and* practices that are ethical. Programs need to be titled and developed as ethics and compliance programs.

Compliance programs fail because they are too often separated from ethical behaviour, and most importantly they are just "words, words,

words"! Research indicates the following as reasons behind the failure of compliance programs:

- Lack of top-level leadership on ethical practices and the importance of compliance policies, with Enron being the classic example, which, as irony would have it, also had an award-winning code of conduct!

- Lack of consistency or monitoring of the policies and procedures. Ethical practices and compliance need constant reinforcement, training, fairness, and consequences.

- Competing resources: either the programs and training/ communication are underfunded, or worse still, ignored due to pressure for achievement of financial targets and response to competitive pressure (like Wells Fargo).

These lead to what is known as the "Fraud Triangle":

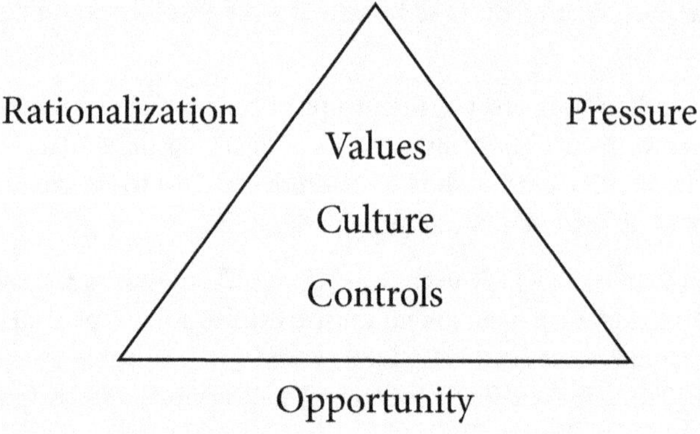

The external elements of the triangle are what influence the internal and increase the likelihood of unethical practice occurring. The internal elements are matched against the external pressures, and together they provide the ethical balance in decision making, leadership, and active compliance policies and practice. Controls (with a focus on compliance policy) are only one third of the balance needed.

Key takeaways on effective ethics and compliance that incorporates the ethical values are:

- Integrity based: focus on the ethical values of the organization;

- Develop a professional identity for the employee and the team that incorporates ethical decision making;

- Relieve the pressure (external and managerial) by seeking newer and better balanced internal solutions;

- Promote a "speak up" culture.

CPA Speaker #4: Prof. Krista Fiolleau PhD. School of Accounting & Finance, University of Waterloo. Director of the Centre for Accounting Ethics. 10 + years in academe subsequent to Areva Resources working as an accountant.

"Behavioural Ethics: Ethical Traps of Our Minds"

Decision-making models are idealized: Too often they ignore the contextual reality of the decision situation. This is at the heart of ethical traps in decision making.

Research from Daniel Kahneman and others indicates two models:

- System 1: intuitive, quick, associative: used 95% of the time.

- System 2: deliberative, slow: used 5% of the time. This is the area most ethics education has focused on.

System 1 is highly practical but often does not result in fully considered judgments so often needed in ethical decision making. An example of these rationalizations is known as "the Dead Presidents Effect" where we often will think it is okay to take (steal) a pen or chocolate bar, but not money. Our minds will often rationalize a pen as immaterial so it is not really theft: "it's immaterial," "I earned it," "everybody is doing it." Money signals value so is seen as different.

There are a number of traps and concepts in behavioural ethics that are important:

- "Bounded ethicality": We try to be ethical in our lives but we are bounded in our ability to reason through our decisions. We can't get all the information, have pre-existing beliefs, are focused on a performance goal and so on. Additionally, we don't like to revisit our mistakes so that learning is limited and bounds our reality further.

- "Conformity bias": A tendency to want to "stick with the crowd," or agreeing so as to avoid tension in the group, or under time pressure so we avoid bringing new data/thinking.

- "Incrementalism": Small ethical issues can often escalate to more serious ones so small unethical decisions start a "slippery slope."

- "Overconfidence bias": Humans are generally overconfident about their own knowledge and skills (e.g., driving skills), which results in not seeking alternative paths or additional education.

- Other behavioural ethics concerns include framing bias, implicit bias, loss aversion, moral myopia, and self-serving bias.

So what can be done to avoid these traps?

- When feeling pressure or things don't feel right, trust your instincts to stop and think.

- Review and re-examine progress and effects of projects and policies: especially during periodic reviews.

- Expand the discussion to other stakeholders (who might be impacted) and other organization goals (reputation, HR issues, etc.).

- Encourage diversity in thinking to block "group think": team diversity, functional diversity, outsiders to bring fresh perspective.

- Moral reminders: Be aware of ethical practices from religion, charities, community groups, company values, and vision statements. Use pictures, videos, live meetings, etc., as well as text.

- The "light of day" test: how would a decision look when reported?

- Don't hide talk about ethics and its importance.

- Stop and reflect: What kind of a person do we want to be? build in some time in your schedule to do this.

CPA Speaker #5: Prof. Robert Steinbauer PhD. Professor of Business Ethics, Goodman School of Business, Brock University. 8+ years in academe following ERC Consultant with Deloitte in the United States.

"Why Good People Make Bad Decisions: Ethics Cheating Scandals and Ethics Training"

Research indicates that about 25% of people lie on a frequent basis, 75% of people are low frequency liars—and 90% of this latter group engage in "white lies" (harmless or trivial to avoid hurting another's feelings).

Why do people lie or cheat? It's a combination of individual differences and the environment. For example, men cheat more than women, younger people cheat more than mature ones. Also, employees with low locus of control over their jobs cheat/lie more than those with more control. However, a more ethical work culture does reduce the level of cheating and a toxic environment increases it.

A positive organization culture/environment is therefore important, as it can prevent "moral disengagement" by the individual. Bad cultures provide an excuse for the employee not to apply their own moral standards:

- There is a diffusion of responsibility: Others do it, so why not me!

- Some see it as not as bad as other things they have heard of: They see an advantageous comparison.

- Blame is attached to the organization culture due to a lack of focus on ethics and over focus on achievement of performance goals.

- It is not seen as the employee's responsibility: displacement of responsibility.

- There are minimal consequences.

- The issue is labeled euphemistically: disguised in a language with no ethical criticism.

With so much business focus on performance and financial goals and pressure to achieve these, a change in mindset is required from a fixed mindset of pass/fail to one that focuses more on learning and growth:

- Instead of just achieve/not achieve performance/finance goals, have growth and learning goals.

- Transform fail into FAIL: First Attempt in Learning. Mistakes should be seen as necessary and shared to encourage learning.

To build this learning and ethical culture requires:

- The importance of corporate mission, vision, and values to be complete and ambitious morally and financially, and regularly shared with ongoing training.

- Adapt the method of learning of ethics and compliance to the backgrounds and learning styles of each employee.

CPA Speaker #6: Prof. Kelly Richmond Pope PhD. Professor School of Accountancy and MIS at De Paul University, Chicago, USA for 16 years. Previously with Red Flag Mania Inc and the Greater Chicago Food Depository. Author of "Fool Me Once" and filmmaker of "All the Queens Horses" on whistleblowers and fraud cases.

"White Collar Crime and Fraud Issues"

In dealing with fraud, insider threats account for 75% of all security breaches. PWC research in 2020 found that organization fraud was 70% accounted for by external attack, or collusion between somebody inside the organization and somebody outside. The reasons employees engage is that they rationalize fraud differently and report it differently. Employees have a cognitive bias where preconception of fraud or not fraud is caused by their own mental short cuts in judgement. This is caused by the System 1 type of thinking discussed earlier and with it the rapid processing of existing information (availability bias), and the halo effect ascribed to certain roles, positions and people. In addition, the legality of an issue like fraud may either not be known or not clear.

Fraud archetypes can be classified as follows:

- Perpetrators

- Intentional (can be planned up front or evolved)

- Accidental (following orders)

- Righteous (use their position to help out others)

Prey

- Innocent bystanders

- Targeted

Whistleblowers

- Accidental (notice something unusual and report it)

- Noble (see something wrong and report it)

- Vigilante (those looking to find fault or to "right a wrong")

There are also crossover motivations.

How to change or block fraud:

- Train staff frequently on policies and procedures and "red flag" occurrences;

- Self-reflect with stories and graphic illustration (e.g., impact of drunk driving accidents)

- Engage external inspection

- Be sure all executives and staff are aware of both risk and consequences.

Reputation Issues: Cases and Viewpoints #2.2. Enron Corporation

Probably the largest, most complicated, and most notorious financial scandal had to do with the Enron Corporation, which was a US-based energy, commodities, and service company. At its peak in mid-2001 the company's shares were trading at a high of US$90.75. By the time the scandal was unveiled by November of that year, they were down to $0.26.

The essence of the issue was that through use of deceptive accounting reporting Enron was able to trick investors into thinking that the company was performing much better than it was.

The principal method employed by Enron to falsify its accounts was to use an accounting method known as mark-to-market (MTM). Under MTM assets can be recorded in company accounts at their fair market value as opposed to book value. Fair market values are hard to determine, and even the then CEO described them as "black box" numbers. In Enron's case these significantly exaggerated the value of the assets.

In addition, under MTM Enron also listed their cash flows that might result from new property, plant, and equipment based on their projections. The actual cash flows that resulted from these assets were substantially less than those reported to the US Securities and Exchange Commission (SEC) in an attempt to hide the losses.

In addition, senior management at Enron orchestrated a scheme to use off-balance-sheet special purpose vehicles (SPVs), also known as special purposes entities (SPEs), to hide Enron's mountains of debt and toxic assets from investors and creditors. The primary aim of these SPVs was to hide accounting realities.

As Enron senior management bonuses were tied to stock price, and some remuneration was in company stock, management was incented to improve stock price and the inflated business results led to inflating the stock price.

Following bankruptcy at the end of 2001, trials and lawsuits continued for some years. While some changes were made to accounting and auditing practice there is still much in the US system of financial regulation that requires due diligence in ethical and compliance attention.

CHAPTER 3
REPUTATION ISSUES: DATA MISUSE OR DATA HACKING

"It is a capital mistake to theorise before one has data. Insensibly one begins to twist facts to suit the theory instead of the theory to suit facts."

– Sir Arthur Conan Doyle; quote taken from the first Sherlock Holmes story, *A Scandal in Bohemia*, from 1891.

In chapter one of her award-winning non-fiction book *Privacy is Power* Carissa Veliz describes how virtually every activity we engage in feeds data to some organization in our "data economy." Whether or not this data is sourced and used depends on our perceived value as a consumer, an employee, an employer, a commuter, a patient, a parent, a friend, a criminal, an immigrant, a spokesperson or influencer, an investor, a taxpayer, a citizen, and so on. In what she calls our "surveillance society" this increasing collection of personal data: "…was born out of the collaboration between private and public institutions. The government allows corporate data collection to thrive so it could make a copy of the data."

Enabled by the tech communications industry with huge players like Apple, Microsoft, Alphabet, Amazon, Tencent, Meta, Alibaba, and

"

others, our data is sourced and analyzed to the benefit of private and public organizations in their work. Often this sourcing is done without the active knowledge of the source. Even when we are conscious of the sourcing, we accept it, as it provides service or products of value in the communications and commerce of our lives. Increasingly though, despite the limited protection provided by legislation, we push back against this data collection and utilization. When that happens, the organizations involved suffer reputational damage and sometime even legal penalties.

In June 2022 the Office of the Privacy Commissioner of Canada concluded that the "Tim Hortons app violated privacy laws in collection of 'vast amounts' of sensitive location data."

Customers downloading the Tim Hortons app had their movements tracked and recorded every few minutes of every day even when the app was not open. The Office concluded this was in violation of Canadian privacy laws. The publicity was widespread and measurably damaged Tim Hortons' reputation.

The most famous—infamous—example is the 2010–2018 Cambridge Analytica incident. In deriving data for political campaigning, Cambridge Analytica developed an app called "This is your Digital Life" and got 270,000 Facebook users to download it. Cambridge Analytica paid a small sum to have respondents complete a psychometric survey. Using the combination of Facebook contacts and data from the questionnaires they then researched and compiled data on some 87 million Facebook users. Then, applying data-backed analytics they developed predictive models on voting and other behaviours and sold them. Issues like Brexit in the UK and political campaigns in the US (e.g., Texas congressional elections) were customers. Though the organization closed in 2018, its impacts still resound.

Pretty well all communication tech companies have had data misuse issues whether by corrupt or poor practice or hacking. Twitter, for example, allowed advertiser access to data without user permission. Google was fined in France for bad practice. Other organizations have also had poor practices or been hacked like Marriott in 2020 and Chapters Indigo in Canada in 2023 that had its customer accounts hacked.

Compliance

Globally, legislative bodies are introducing stronger data privacy legislation. It is not an easy task as the balance between required data protection and over-oppressive government interference is difficult to strike.

In Canada in 2022/2023 Bill C-27 (44-1), known as the Digital Charter Information Act, is in legislative process to update existing legislation of the Consumer Privacy Protection Act, the Personal Information and Data Protection Tribunal Act and the Artificial Intelligence and Data Act. In the US myriad state-based data privacy laws exist, but there's no country-wide legislation. In the European Union (EU) the General Data Protection Registration (GDPR) was adopted in 2016 and applied since 2018. It is generally regarded as the strongest data protection legislation in the world and is a model for the Canadian Bill C-27. The EU is going further. The GDPR is adopting new regulation, which will mostly be in place by the end of 2023 includes the following:

- The Data Governance Act creates a new way of managing data to increase trust in, and facilitate data sharing.

- The Digital Markets Act creates fair and contestable markets for innovation, growth and competitiveness in the digital sector.

- The Digital Services Act creates a safer digital space where the rights of all users of digital services are protected.

- The Data Act regulates access to data in B2B, B2C, and B2G (business to government) relationships and while switching between cloud providers.

- The AI Act enacts stringent regulations of high-risk AI systems, and prohibition of certain practices.

As the McKinsey March 1st commentary on "The EU Digital Strategy" comments, "There are new possibilities and benefits from the new regulatory regime." These include better and more legitimate data sharing and portability, reducing the market power of gatekeepers, and better protection of end-user rights, especially with regard to AI.

Data Misuse

Today a wide range and number of organizations have access to our personal information: demographics, spending patterns, beliefs and attitudes, and our family and friendship networks. These days it is now the case that virtually every organization that we interact with has access to our personal information. Often the data has been given voluntarily. Quite understandably marketers want to know more about the target groups they market to, and their target groups want to receive better service and information from them. The danger for both marketers and the public is when this data is collected without permission, applied outside of any permission, combined with other data without permission, and in general used in a manner not consistent with respect for someone's privacy.

The business and reputational risk for marketers is that their customers start withholding data, move to brands that are less intrusive, and/or take action publicly or legally against the brand. Data misuse can be seen in the following ways:

1. Excessive data requested/required: For fairly straightforward transactions an excessive amount of data is requested. On line credit card data for event/restaurant reservations is an example.

2. Gaining personal data from other than the individual: For example, having children respond to data requests about themselves or their family.

3. Commingling: Data derived for a specific purpose is reviewed/ used without consent for another purpose. Often the data is combined with data from another source.

4. Brand data used for personal benefit: Where employees transfer brand data for personal or non-specific brand use.

5. Ambiguity: Where the request for data from the user is intentionally or unintentionally ambiguous. This enables broader use of the data than the provider is aware.

6. Inadequate or misleading consent agreements for data access and use.

As for number 6, there is a big difference between expressed consent and informed consent. Too often consent agreements are too long, confusing, over-legalistic. The intent is often to confuse the individual or make it too time consuming and complex to be considered for its ramifications. Individuals faced with access to a small product or service advantage are signing away far too intrusive rights of access to information and data about themselves.

A current example in the US has emerged with the potential merger of the Kroger supermarket organization (sales of $137 billion in 35 states in the US), with Albertsons (sales of $72 billion) being investigated by the Federal Trade Commission. It is not just the grocery shopping impact being investigated but data privacy issues as well. Kroger has extensive subsidiaries engaged in data collection, analysis, and their sale through its companies 84:51, Kroger Precision Marketing, Kroger Personal Finance, and Dunnhumby. Their privacy policy is so broad as to be meaningless: "…we only collect information when needed for a particular purpose." The data they collect from their loyalty programs like Kroger Plus and Kroger Boost covers over

2,000 variables and include:

- Personal and demographic information;

- Purchase data;

- Store locations and internal store areas visited;

- Credit details;

- Health information drawn from products purchased;

- Behavioural influences; and

- Some biometric information like facial recognition based on filmed store visits

What often makes this whole issue a difficult issue is the opportunity for better knowledge on which to take legitimate socially appropriate action. Along with others I was faced with this during 2022. As part of a group advising the federal government on gaining optimal Covid-19 vaccination acceptance, we recognised that there were no national health care records. While vaccination was to the benefit of all and knowing people's health status would have enabled a more effective approach, lack of records made the task more difficult and increased the risk of infection to the total population, as became evident in many other countries. As it happens, Canadians sensibly mostly sought vaccination, so our rate of illness and death was lower than most countries, but could it have been even lower with national or even provincially held central records?

The overall issue of privacy and data misuse will become ever more important. The balance between organizations wanting better targeted sales communication and consumers wanting to be served better, and the risks of these organizations knowing too much and abusing the knowledge is a hard one to strike. The risks of getting it wrong will lead to reputational and possible financial and legal damage. In any ethics and compliance policy this area needs research, thought, and training that should focus more on the ethical treatment of people than just compliance.

Cases and Viewpoints #3: Data Management Tool

So what can organizations do?

1. Establish a data collection and management policy.

    - As part of this process, be clear about what data on customers, prospects, and competitive customers you need;

    - Identify sources, and credibility, of this data;

    - Based on this, establish a draft policy on what you are prepared to do to collect the information and what your corporate values restrain;

    - Work with your ethics & compliance advisors on legal and ethical restraints to collecting and using the data required;

    - Work with your IT advisors on IT changes, opportunities, and ethical and compliance dangers of improvements in data collection;

    - Develop a final data-management policy.

2. Develop and act on a briefing and training plan for the whole organization starting with the finance, HR, legal and compliance and marketing and sales departments.

3. Develop the guidelines in straightforward language. Avoid overcomplicated legalese and ensure multilingual versions are available for diverse staff.

4. Review the planned data use and privacy agreements with consumers/customers/employees to ensure they are adequate yet understandable without extensive legal training.

5. Review this policy:

    - With all new employees;

    - When there is any change in compliance standards or issues raised by customers and prospects;

    - With all staff on a regular basis e.g., every six months.

Also, include this policy and its updates in yearly senior management and Board meetings.

CHAPTER 4
REPUTATION ISSUES: VIRAL CUSTOMER COMPLAINTS FOR POOR SERVICE AND/ OR TREATMENT

"Your most unhappy customers are your greatest source of learning."

– Bill Gates, American business person, co-founder Microsoft

In this age of social media, news of bad customer service experiences is transmitted quickly and widely. The key to managing reputation protection is to avoid:

- Service events that cause significant negative customer impact.

- Frequent repetition of the same or similar events.

- Unreasonable explanations of why the bad service has occurred is given to customers.

- Lack of any explanation and/or apology from the organization and its individual staff members.

- Not providing suitable compensation for the customer when warranted.

- Perceived, or real, price gouging.

Service

In any organization there will always be errors or lapses in customer service. The goal is to set standards, budgets, and staff motivation and training to avoid incidents causing problems outlined above.

A significant cause of these problems in an over 70% of gross domestic product (GDP) service economy that lies in management failing to achieve a positively directed, trained, knowledgeable, motivated workforce. As such, management of this issue is largely dependent on effective management of staff to avoid a toxic organizational culture and remuneration biases (for a ranking of Canada's best employers see Cases and Viewpoints #5.1. in Chapter 5). While labour cost in a number of industries is a key financial issue, issues of equity, skill and motivation of staff increasingly take strategic priority. In terms of customer service these are all key issues not only for business performance but for ethical and compliance reasons:

- Equity: Ensuring that job descriptions define pay and benefits not gender, ethnic background or sexual orientation;

- Skill: Providing training and development for staff, not just in their current role, but opportunities for development and promotion;

- Motivation: Providing a work environment and culture where staff are motivated at their work and provide high quality customer service.

While a poorly motivated staff are an issue in poor customer service, it is not the only reason. Other issues also provide primary explanation:

- Poor or insufficient knowledge or motivation by senior management as to the importance of good customer service in achieving organizational objectives and in managing the reputation of the organization. Too often the financial objectives are too short term or how they are to be achieved. Also, the role of customer satisfaction is not sufficiently understood.

- Poor or inadequate policies as to customer service: lack of definition of what is expected in terms of everyday delivery and how to handle problems.

- Even where policies do exist, poor or inadequate staff training in how to assess the issue, implement, communicate and follow-up with customers.

- Insufficient funds to handle everyday customer service requirements, errors, and problems.

- Poor organization design where organization silos or hierarchy restrict ability to resolve customer service issues quickly and effectively.

- Poor organization technology that restricts communication and response capability in handling customer service issues.

- A poorly motivated staff due to a poor employee culture and/or insufficient attention and reward given for good/great customer service.

Organizations will occasionally deliver poor customer service: In any human-to-human contact errors or lack of consideration will occur. Poor or broken technology adds to the potential problems. In addition, some customers have unrealistic expectations. However, to thrive in the 21st century organizations need to avoid major and frequent negative customer service issues. Some industries are frequent offenders in delivering poor customer service:

- Airlines. They have been particularly troubled with cancellations, delays, baggage delivery, inadequate communication of issues and action, and other problems. While weather does cause some of these issues, the industry has been universally bad in addressing the problems. The impact has been seen in increasing legislative action: in Canada the 2019 Air Passenger Protection Regulation (AAPR) passed and in September 2022 was extended. Due to airline misinformation about causes like weather, this remains a contentious issue. Additionally, the slow rate of response to service problems has added to the poor reputation of many, if not most, airlines. In Canada recently Sunwing has been a particular example although others like Air Transat, Air Canada and Westjet have not been free of criticism. In the US, Spirit Airlines and United Airlines have been a particular focus of criticism.

- Telecommunications. The oligopoly of Bell, Rogers, and Telus hasn't fared well when it comes to reputation or customer service studies. Despite some legislative supervision, the lack of choice and differentiated service mean customers feel they have little choice. In the US, AT&T, Comcast and Sprint do not fare well.

- Financial Services. While the top banks in Canada—BMO, CIBC, Desjardins, National Bank, RBC, Scotiabank and TD—are not loved for customer service, they are trusted by Canadians. In recent years they have made major strides in improving staff relationships and technology, which has helped mitigate against the worst reputation for customer service. Major credit unions like VanCity and Meridiantend are more highly regarded. Insurance companies like Cooperators, Great West Lifeco, Intact, Manulife, and Sun Life tend to have trusted but not great customer service reputations. US organizations show similar patterns with Equifax and Wells Fargo frequently receiving criticism for poor customer service.

- Retail. In Canada some retailers like Shoppers Drug Mart, Canadian Tire, Home Depot, and Costco elicit high customer service ratings. (Cases and Viewpoints #4.1. Leger Corporate Reputation Survey 2023 at the end of this chapter.) They tend to have positive employee cultures and remuneration programs that aid the service ratings.

In general, organizations like Apple, GE, Google, Suntory, and Toyota have consistently good customer service reputations.

Price Gouging

In the recent period of increased inflation, criticism from customers over price increases has arisen. While organizations like IT companies; raw material suppliers (lithium, cobalt, copper, nickel, aluminium); retailers; restaurants; and others have increased prices to cover increased labour and supply costs, and received negative media comments for doing so, these are not the extreme issues that cause the most harm. Excessive prices and/or price increases are too often caused by greed and opportunism from senior management as a way to take advantage of monopolistic or oligopolistic situations. These opportunities look tempting in the short term, but cause damage reputationally and sometimes legally.

An infamous recent example was Valeant Pharmaceutical in the 2011–2016 period. With a near monopoly on its Calcium EDTA drug as a treatment for lead poisoning, in one year the management increased the price by 2,700%! Management then used these and other inflated earnings forecasts to attract investors. Valeant then experience legal action for price fixing and then misleading financial information by the US Securities and Exchange Commission and others and is now out of business with assets acquired by others. Not illegal, but a further example of reputationally damaging price gouging is the "dynamic ticket pricing" policy of Ticketmaster. Its pricing based on demand per concert, this organization acts like ticket touts/scalpers in selling tickets for concerts by such performers as Bruce Springsteen and Harry Stiles. Additionally, as reported by the CBC TV Marketplace program, in a number of regions (e.g., Niagara Falls tourist area) some organizations are adding fees to invoices and bills rather than change the base pricing, the implication being that it is some kind of new tax. Under headings like "Daily Hotel Levy," "Luxury Fee," "Niagara Falls Destination Fee (NFDF)," "Tourist Impact Fee" and others, a charge of between 3%–12% is added to the total by the different organizations.

In some cases, this was declared in small print on menus or signs, but in many cases it was not. All the fees collected went to the organization involved. Authorities are examining the legality as well as the ethics of this, although the situation has been evident for a considerable time, with fees increasing considerably post-pandemic. Gift cards are another area where this hidden pricing often occurs. Organizations like The Peoples Group who do gift cards for federally regulated financial institutions often reduce the value of the cards each year if they are not utilized for 12 months.

The point is that while control of supply does enable more upward price flexibility when there are no clear substitutes, taking a "profit maximization" approach to pricing may look attractive for one product or service. However, it is likely to cause reputational damage and financial damage across the whole organization, and its operations and may be subject to legal action or government intervention.

Summary

Organizations that pay attention to good customer service and fair pricing practices do not just benefit by avoiding reputationally damaging stories, they acquire positive business results. Depending on the industry, research indicates that about 65% of company business comes from repeat customers; 86% of customers with great service experience will shop from that company/brand again; and Bain research indicates a 5% increase in customer retention can boost profitability by 25%–96% depending on the industry. There are equally decisive statistics for the negative. (helpscout.ca blog of November 28, 2022, has an assembly of relevant statistics).

The point is that proper strategic and operational attention to achieving great customer service and avoiding frequent poor customer treatment result in positive reputational and business results.

Cases and Viewpoints #4.1:
A Consumer View and a
Researcher's View.

Each year Leger Research does consumer research on which brands/ companies have a positive reputation. While limited to B2C, not B2B, relationships, it gives an idea of where organization brands stand in the consumer's mind. The first part of this case are concerned with 2023 survey results. The second part is an interview with Dave Scholz, Chief Strategy Officer, Leger.

Leger Corporate Reputation Study 2023.

In its 26th year of research, the Leger Corporate Reputation Study– April 2023 had the following process and results. Each year, reputation is driven by general socio-economic and ethical concerns as well as specific corporate issues. In 2022/23 the strong overall influencers were inflation, interest rate hikes, and the consumer search for value which had strong influence on sectors like grocery, telecommunications, transportation, and banking.

Of the top 299 companies in Canada evaluated for reputation, awareness, and good minus bad opinion, the average score approximately +25%, in a theoretical range of +100% to -100%. Fieldwork through November 2022 and January 2023 included a sample of 39,000 people, with each person rates 2,100. Only 50 brands out of almost 300 evaluated receive a net positive score.

Over net +50% n= 50 brands:

Top Ten

Google (+75%), Sony, Shoppers Drug Mart, Samsung, Canadian Tire, YouTube, Dollarama, Home Depot, Costco, Campbell (+67%).

Remaining Top Forty

Microsoft, A&W, Staples, Kellogg, Kraft Heinz, McCain, Interac, Best Buy, IKEA, Toyota, Amazon, Canada Post, Netflix, Maple Leaf, Marks, Cirque du Soleil, LG, Panasonic, Honda, CAA, Tim Hortons, Subway, Visa, FedEx, Mastercard, Winners, Hilton, Purolator, Danone, Home

Hardware, Marriott, Apple, Sobeys, General Mills, Chapters Indigo Michaels Sheraton, UPS, Nestle, and Wendy's.

Others:

n=249 brands including 7 with net negative (B2Bs not measured).

2. Interview with Dave Scholz, Chief Strategy Officer, Leger.

The increasing importance and value of the study has been driven by three forces:

1. The actionability of the research that directly asks consumers about their opinion (good or bad) of the organization if they are aware of it.

2. The ability for organizations to source from the research a fuller understanding of reputational issues of the specific organization and its sector.

3. The rise of social media and with it a huge rise in reputation-influencing stories about organizations and its people and practices.

Guided by the ongoing work of James E. Grunig, following his 1992 work *Excellence in Public Relations and Communications Management*, Dave Scholz agrees with the concept of "controlled mutuality" whereby all organizations suffer ups and downs in reputation, but understanding the ability and credibility of the parties to influence each other helps them formulate effective communications strategies. As Dave says, "If I care about you (the organization) then I am likely to listen to your viewpoint."

The necessary understanding includes clarity and consistency of ethical value standards in the organization, full briefing and training of all staff, effective management of reputational information—both positive and negative—about the organization, and as Dave says, most importantly, *"Organizations have to be more transparent, more genuine, more visible, and not just in defense and managing crises. They must now actively engage with key audiences."*

He also points out the importance of measurement of both the good and bad aspects of reputation: *"That key reputational measures based on surveys like the Reputation Study are an essential part of its management."*

Dave goes on to add: *"That, now, reputation management is a Board and C-suite responsibility. It hasn't always been. Corporate name and their brand names must be considered together at the highest level."*

Interview: April 6, 2023

CHAPTER 5
REPUTATION ISSUES: TOXIC ORGANIZATION CULTURE AND EMPLOYMENT/WAGE BIAS

"Take care of Associates and they'll take care of your customers."

– J. William Marriott, 1932, American former Chair of the Board of Marriott International

"Happy employees create happy customers who buy more, creating more profits, and recommend the organization to others. Research has found a strong correlation between employee and customer happiness. Financial results are a proxy of how well the organization has created value for employees and customers."

– Elliot S. Schreiber in *The Yin and Yang of Reputation Management*

Throughout my academic career teaching marketing I always discussed marketing's constituent elements as the "5 x Ps," not "4 x Ps," needed to build a strong brand. Marketing decisions must include a blended approach to:

- The Product or service being offered:

- The Place or the distribution strategy for delivering the product/service to the customer;

- The Promotion or blend of marketing communications to promote the brand;

- The Pricing charged for the brand;

- The People delivering the service or working in the organization on the brand and its activities.

That fifth "P" of people has always been an essential element whether the brand is product or service or a B2C or B2B offering. As such it is not surprising that how organization employees or contract partners are treated and the values and culture of the organization have such a powerful effect on the reputation of the overall organization and its brands. As evidenced in the previous chapter, the customer service provided is a key feature in reputation management. This chapter discusses how workforce culture and relationships are themselves so important in the reputation of the organization and its brand(s).

The reasons the internal environment and culture of an organization become toxic differ between organizations, but here are some of the characteristics:

- Lack of attention to the values and culture of the organization by senior management and the Board in policies and practice.

- Outdated employment practices that ignore the DEI principles and practice of Diversity, Equity, and Inclusion.

- "Mass layoffs/hire and fire" practices by senior management (e.g., in late 2022/early 2023: Amazon, Dell, Disney/ESPN, DoorDash,

Facebook, Goldman Sachs, Google, Microsoft, PayPal, Peloton, Snapchat, Spotify, Zoom and others). Bad management practice in over-hiring, then firing led to between 2% and 25% of these workforces being laid off.

- Frequent conflicts between employees both across and within functions.

- Lack of cooperation across functions and organizational silos.

- Frequent and ongoing conflicts or friction between employees and management.

- Lack of communication between employees on work issues that harm performance or understanding of the job.

- General lack of communication, at any level, that leads to employees feeling isolated, alone, and not knowing where to go for help or advice.

- Employees over-competitive with each other, hoard important information and focus on blame rather than resolution of issues.

- Employees feel they have to work constant overtime in order to retain their jobs or be fairly compensated.

- There are clear disparities in remuneration that seem to be based on age, gender, ethnicity, sexual orientation, and reasons that seemingly have nothing to do with the job description or goal achievement.

- Management does not want to hear about these issues, provides inadequate feedback, or refuses to do anything about them. Failure to listen, measure (like employment Net Promoter Score – eNPS), or act on issues

Overall, this shows up as poor morale, poor performance, and high staff turnover. Poor management ignores the symptoms and do not spend sufficient time, attention, or money on establishing their organizational core values, or working on establishing a positive set of policies for internal promotion and practices. In Canada one of the most noted organizations with toxic workplaces is the RCMP. Numerous investigations including the March 30, 2023, "Mass Casualty Commission" on the Nova Scotia April 2022 shootings have documented a toxic workplace that has led to constant policing errors and problems.

Organizations that have suffered public criticism and/or poor ratings on surveys like Glassdoor on these issues in the US or globally have included Adobe, Amazon, Dyson, Forever 21, Frontier, Hertz, Walmart, and Uber. Those that have been well regarded include Bain, BCG, Cisco, Google, Hubspot and McKinsey. While many organizations continue to perform well for reasons other than corporate culture, many do not and even those that do, face weaknesses in the achievement of their goals.

Elliot Schreiber's *The Yin and Yang of Reputation Management* has as "Principle 1: Values and Culture are principal sources of reputation and risk."

This applies across the total organization and its culture. Culture here is defined as "a set of norms and values that are widely shared and strongly held throughout the organization."

Building from an article in the *Harvard Business Review* of January/February 2018 ("The leaders guide to corporate culture. How to manage the eight critical elements of organizations"), David Kincaid in his book *The Brand Driven CEO* discusses six elements of what he terms the "people ecosystem" that make up organizational culture. Building off these six elements, I have elaborated on them as follows:

1. Organizational Structure: moving away from structures based on hierarchy, function, and paternalism to "a network of teams." In these organizations job roles and responsibilities cross functional silos and focus on goals and rewards reflecting the overall organizational priorities. Skills and learning for all levels of employees are emphasised. As discussed in my earlier book

Mentorship Matters mentoring becomes an important managerial skill. In addition, project management capabilities are increasingly important.

2. Roles & Responsibilities: self-managing teams with opportunities to innovate in achieving their goals are emphasised and rewarded.

3. Culture tracking and management: the hiring, training, and development of employees receives much greater attention and budget. Staff satisfaction, development, and reward is encouraged and staff turnover minimized. I have been lucky enough to experience this environment: first when working in Japan where the ethos of the company HR process was to find the best roles for staff where they could thrive and develop. The other is my local restaurant in Toronto, "Hot House," where staff are treated well so they remain there, get to know the customers and therefore where the customers receive excellent service and attention.

4. Hiring and Feedback Practices: recruiting people not only for existing skills but the interest and ability to be developed further. In addition, diversity of background and importantly what I call "humanity"; Jacinda Ardern, the ex-Prime Minister of New Zealand, calls this caring: "be strong and be kind." This means an equal emphasis on goal achievement and an interest in others and their role and personality. Once hired, management's responsibility is to train, explain, and retain. As David Kincaid says, "Employees want to know how their job and the work they do contribute to the success of the organization."

5. Training and Development: this needs not only to be in the specific job function but a broader capability and one that stimulates thinking and job enrichment. Sadly, Canada does not do well in the time and money our organizations spend in this area. As I know from my time in management education, surveys like IMD's World Talent Ranking (2022; sample of 63 countries) indicate that Canada ranks only #8 in management education and #11 in "competent senior managers."

6. Compensation and Incentives: compensation plans should reward employees: "According to their achievement of desired brand values and behaviors as well as business results." (David Kincaid). Additionally, incentives and recognition should reflect goal achievement of not only themselves but the team. Recognition needs to be important but meaningful to people, not a routine.

The point is that an organization's values and culture are now key elements in the achievement of success and in protecting and advancing an organization's reputation. Each of the areas outlined above need to be addressed to avoid dysfunctional and toxic workplaces that harm performance and reputation.

Cases and Viewpoints #5.1: Canada's Best Employers

There are many surveys of employers based on employee recommendations. I have included two in this section.

One I have chosen is conducted by Forbes/Statistica, as it includes non-business employers and represents the reality of the employment market and with it a view on the health of the organizational culture. The 2023 survey is amongst 12,000 employees of organizations with over 500 employees.

Respondents were asked on a 1–10 scale how likely they were to recommend their organization to others. Here are the top 50 organizations in the 2023 survey:

Top Ten

Sheridan College, Canadian Mental Health Association, The Keg Steakhouse and Bar, Ericsson, Export Development Canada, Carleton University, Hydro-Quebec, Cisco Systems, Microsoft, OpenText.

11–20

Shared Health, Grant Thornton, McMaster University, Lululemon Athletica, Pratt & Whitney, Concordia University, Google, City of Brampton, PCL Construction, BC Hydro.

21–30

Coca-Cola Bottling, The Co-operators, Mercedes-Benz, University of Victoria, Regional Municipality of York, Children's Hospital of Eastern Ontario, Bank of Canada, American Express, City of Markham.

31–40

University of Manitoba, IKEA, Manitoba Hydro, Sephora, Desjardins, University of New Brunswick, British Columbia Institute of Technology, Health Canada, Advanced Micro Devices, University of British Columbia.

41–50

Ontario Lottery and Gaming, Dalhousie University, Agnico Eagle

Mines, Canada Revenue Agency, Subway, Purolator, ArcelorMittal Dofasco, Advantage Solutions, Honda Motor, Laval University.

Another study is one done by Leger as part of their yearly Corporate Reputation Study. In the 2023 report questions on employer reputation were asked. This was based on respondent assessments of the organization's attractiveness as employers.

Four dimensions were questioned: perceived atmosphere (does it seem a good place to work); future potential (are there good employment opportunities); attractiveness of the business (future potential for the business); and values (do the values of the business seem attractive). Additionally, respondents were asked if they felt they had the qualifications to be employed.

The top ten ranked employers in this survey were:

Samsung, Toyota, Costco, Shoppers Drug Mart, Microsoft, Google, Sony, Home Depot, Apple, and Honda.

All top ten were similar to previous years.

CHAPTER 6
REPUTATION ISSUES: LACK OF CLARITY, COMMUNICATION, UNDERSTANDING OR TRAINING IN ETHICAL AND COMPLIANCE BEHAVIOUR BY ALL STAFF LEVELS

"Human behaviour flows from three main sources: desire, emotion, and knowledge."

– Plato, 428–348 BCE, Philosopher, Athens, Greece

In reviewing the issues that damage reputation—poor, misleading or illegal financial management; data misuse and data hacking; viral customer complaints for poor service and/or treatment; toxic organizational culture and remuneration biases—it is essential that comprehensive and actionable policies *and* practices are required. Too often policies supported by a Board of Directors, CEO, COO, and senior management are inadequate. Case history evidence suggests that even where policies exist practice of those policies is inadequate. Too often the fault lies in inadequate communication of policies and insufficient or inadequate training and follow up.

Reputation management in this era of social media and twenty-first century ethical standards is not just about avoiding negatives but encouraging humane, inclusionary, and ethical practices. Reputation management is about building a positive reputation not just about avoiding a negative. Both positive and negative outcomes have financial impacts and so are KSFs (Key Success Factors) in organizational achievement.

Action Plan

What actions should organizations take? Clearly it will depend on the organization's business and current policies and practices, but in general the following represents a coherent process:

First and most importantly, the Board of Directors, CEO, COO .and senior management need to understand and enthusiastically agree on the importance of having clear ethics and compliance as well as risk management policies guiding organization objectives, strategy, and practice. Support and engagement on this can be led by the chief ethics and legal executive but it is a task that must be shared and agreed by the whole senior management and enshrined in a Board overview.

In his book Elliot Schreiber suggests that a new type of Board committee be formed: a Strategy and Stakeholder Value Board Committee. This committee would assume responsibility for oversight of senior management on risk, ethics, and compliance and reputation management for the risks outlined earlier in this book.

Second, having decided to go ahead and develop policies and procedures a management group should be formed: a Strategy and Stakeholder Value Executive Committee. This group should not only include experts in legal/compliance issues and social and ethical standards, but also representatives of the different organizational functions. At minimum it should include the CEO and/or COO, CFO, Chief HR Officer, Chief Legal and Ethics and Compliance Officer, Chief Operations Officer and Chief Marketing Officer. Importantly this group should also regularly call on front line staff as well as management so that a complete and realistic strategy can be developed (note the importance of this emphasised earlier in Emmanuel Lulin's Case 1.1). As part of this process the learning can be used to revise organization design and processes to be more effective, efficient, and engaging for the staff.

Third, after the recommendation is reviewed and discussed, the policies should be passed by both the Board on behalf of shareholders and senior management in order to establish clear direction. Sufficient time should be allowed and announced for activation. Follow-up reviews should be planned to respond to changes in legislation, social practice, or response to reputational, ethical and compliance issues experienced.

Fourth, in writing up the policies and procedures the language needs to be clear and user friendly. As such the employee write-up needs to be clear not only in ethnic language but it also needs to be written in an easy-to-comprehend style. Language that's too legalistic will block understanding. Therefore, the policies and procedures need to be short and easy to understand. Additionally, stories and examples taken from real world instances should be included as examples.

Fifth, communication of the policies and procedures should be done in person in meetings and training sessions that allow discussion and questioning. These should be conducted regularly. All new employees should review them as part of onboarding. At the review meetings, feedback on positives and negatives should be discussed and handed on to the executive(s) in charge of the department and/ or program. Management education should include training and programs and seminars offered by organizations like the CPA (see

Cases and Viewpoints #2.1 earlier in this book) and also the HEC Business School (see Cases and Viewpoints #6.1 at the end of this chapter; as a note for full disclosure, I am an Associate Professor of HEC).

Sixth, there should be a regular report back to all staff on the policies, procedures, feedback, and stories from staff. Organizations should consider including attention to these in personnel reviews. The point is to have the organization staff "living" the positive culture of the organization and contributing to it. There will be a natural human bias to emphasise good reports and stories but the reports should also be clear about instances of poor behaviour and the learning from it.

Seventh, overview of policies, practices, and results should be included in corporate annual reports and other organizational publicity material. Increasingly shareholders, governments, influencers, current, and potential employees and media of all forms want to know not just the financial results but how the policies, practices, values, and culture of the organization achieved them.

Reputation Issues – Cases and Viewpoints #6.1: HEC Montreal Certification in Ethics and Compliance.

In 2019 the Executive Education team at HEC Business School at the University of Montreal recognised the challenges both Quebec-based and Canadian organizations were having with their reputations caused by breaches in acceptable legal compliance and ethical behaviours. Drawing on faculty from HEC, University of Montreal, and guest instructors from industry they designed and launched an Eight–day Open Program.

They attracted sponsors from the CDPQ, Hydro Quebec, Osler, KPMG, and Desjardins and a highly engaged and large audience for at least two or three programs per year. The course blended legal, operational, and managerial perspectives in the following modules:

Module 1: Fundamentals of Ethics and Compliance

- Regulatory Framework

- Applied Ethics

- Ethics and Compliance from Theory to Practice

Module 2: Compliance Function and Program

- Organizational Leadership and Culture

- The Role of Governance in Organizational Ethics

- Compliance Program: Direction and Monitoring

- Internal Investigations

Module 3: Key Topics

- Corporate Fraud

- Corruption

- Global Issues: Fighting Corruption Around the World

- Due Diligence

- Compliance Program Investigations

Module 4: Key Topics

- Cybersecurity and Data Protection

- Preventing Harassment

- Managing Communication in a Crisis Situation

- Role of the Media: Investigation, Journalism and Crisis

- Dealing with Complex Issues

- Exam

Module 5: Case Analysis

- Team case study and presentation to an expert panel

The course receives enthusiastic reviews: two based on interviews with the author illustrate this and the value of the diversity of topics in the program

Attendee #1: Ms. Radosveta Ilieva, Chief of Governance, IT, and communications and compliance management—Hydro Quebec.

Interview September 13, 2022. Attended HEC Montreal Certificate in Ethics and Compliance Fall 2021.

A talented and experienced executive in audit, risk management (ERM), internal control, and especially IT ethics and compliance. In addition to her current role, Radosveta previously worked in these roles at Loto Quebec, ISAC Montreal, Cogeco, and Ernst & Young. She has a Bachelors in Public Accounting from HEC.

After two years in her role at Hydro Quebec, Radosveta was looking for a course that broadened her knowledge and experience.

"In the GRC world (Governance, Risk, Compliance) *I was looking for a program offering compliance certification. Mostly in my career we talk about risk, we talk about controls, we talk about audit but compliance not that much, and ethics not that much too. My question was how do I bring all this in IT."*

Radosveta is primarily responsible for IT ethics and compliance for her 3,500 people out of the 22,000 employees of Hydro Quebec. This involves organizing, training, encouraging, and measuring these policies and practices. In assessing the risks and behaviors and setting up effective policies and practices she works with the legal department responsible for the Hydro Quebec code of ethics, the general compliance team, the audit team, and other departments.

Hydro Quebec had central compliance teams in the legal department but it was not so well developed in IT.

"There was a compliance group in IT because we have to be compliant with NERC (North American Electric Reliability Corporation) CIP standards for bulk electricity compliance. But I then expanded this gradually to encompass other sections in the growing importance of IT and to be following the ISO 37001 international standards for the governance of organizations."

The some 22,000 + standards of the ISO have increasingly involved IT issues in privacy and confidentiality as well as anti-corruption issues driven by various pieces of national legislation. As such Radosveta has added such areas as risk and compliance management.

One of the great strengths in the HEC Ethics and Compliance program she attended was that in the group of 10 attendees there were a range of experiences and viewpoints: lawyers working in compliance teams, bankers, police and others:

"The same topic was not viewed through the same lens."

The course offered the opportunity to view the whole arena of ethics and compliance:

"Ethics and compliance: we all use the same words but we all have different reality and those realities are pieces of the whole reality. All of us work in silos and our training is specific, but we need to understand the broader picture. In our groups we discussed this from our different perspectives. This multiplicity I enjoyed a lot."

The different topics were well covered by the faculty: financial statement fraud, corruption, legal requirements of the civil code and others. Not surprisingly, given her responsibilities, Radosveta felt more attention should be given to IT issues in ethics: AI, internet of things, cyber security, data privacy and so on. Indeed, the research in this discipline indicates this as the major area of growth for attention.

She also felt the case analysis and simulation was really good and as they had to present their findings, this should be allotted more time:

"The case/simulation was a Board presentation and we all (attendees) present to

Hydro Quebec is going through a massive transformation currently to create one integrated Hydro Quebec. As IT practices touch everything, Radosveta took an approach to improve breadth and integration of the topics:

"We needed a transverse approach. When I came in, we had different teams following their own specific needs: health and safety, then ISO, then compliance, internal audit and so on. So, we 'put them all in one room' and built an integrated calendars of topics with overlap and action drawn both from the strategic plan and for the established corporate compliance domains like change management; cyber security and the six other domains. We looked at access, controls and operation; continuity management and so on. Then we mapped all the risks and all the requirements including ethics risk. We now have a complete and integrated view for IT. We built a compliance program that included everything including ethics."

This mapping included what was expected, its communication, training, measurement, and follow-up.

"In our risk management we started at the strategic plan, and worked downwards: what do we need to get there, what are the laws to which we have to comply, what are emerging as issues, what is expected reputationally so that reputation risks are fully understood. As a public company these are very important to us."

Radosveta saw the value of the HEC program and its range of topics and its integration of being of value across other groups in the organization like legal. The crossing of silos will be a huge issue in building not only a fully compliant organization but an ethically driven one with effective governance.

To fully get there, she saw an opportunity for a customized but integrated training program across the functions for Hydro Quebec with more tools to take back for implementation.

Attendee #2: Ms. Julie Broullet CPA. Director Costing, Financial Policies and Internal Control; Treasury Board Submission Unit, Financial and Procurement Services, Corporate Management Branch, Canadian Food Inspection Agency/Government of Canada.

Interview September 8, 2022. Attended the HEC Montreal Certificate in Ethics and Compliance program in Fall 2021.

Attendee of the HEC Certificate in Ethics and Compliance program a blended live and online delivery in French: Julie attended online from Ottawa and was highly complementary about the technology and course delivery. Julie Broullet is an executive from the Canadian Food Inspection Agency in Ottawa where she has been for two years. Julie's previous career includes four years with Public Services and Procurement Canada. Before that, she worked with Parks Canada for 10 years following 10 years in financial roles in the private sector with publicly traded organizations.

Julie's employer offered her the opportunity to attend the program as part of a performance review, which she enthusiastically accepted. Her current role engages her directly in ethics and compliance issues:

"Probably 50% of my job. Compared to the private sector, our agency has a very different view of risk and what it means to make ethical decisions. It is not just ethics in terms of finance, but animal treatment, stakeholder management, staff management and so on."

The complexities of ethics and compliance are more complicated in the federal government due to the impact of differing budgets, and myriad stakeholders: the public service, MPs, ministers, other governments domestically and internationally, suppliers, grant and benefit recipients, and of course the public at large.

"It is about compliance but increasingly it's about ethics and ethical practices."

One of the major benefits of the HEC program was the range of backgrounds of the attendees:

"You had the accountants and the auditors, there was also a police officer; there were writers, and then there were lawyers. There were very different perspectives which I really appreciated: the broader perspectives that were not just financial or legal. There was so much value in hearing from

private sector, not-for-profit and public sector perspectives as well: the styles were so different it was great learning."

What particularly appealed to Julie was the leadership topics:

"How do you talk to leaders about ethical issues: ethical decision making and governance."

Julie was less engaged with some of the legal topics, but really loved Crisis Management, the session on corruption, and the links to governance and ethical decision making. Julie was a real enthusiast of these issues in the program, including an understanding of risk, and how these should be developed into helping advance ethical decision making and create a real ethical culture.

"It showed how ethics can become real."

When asked what issues should be covered in more depth either in this program or follow up, Julie quickly and emphatically said:

"Governance."

This needed, in her view, to be covered in more depth. The view is consistent with Julie's view that ethical behaviors and principles need to be part of an organization's overall culture.

"What is the role of governance in making ethics real? The new generation, those under 30 years old, almost find it offensive if the focus is just on minor issues of compliance. It has to be broader. This generation is so much smarter, so if the focus is on minor issues of compliance, they think we are insulting their intelligence. If I was to take another course it would be governance, ethics and how do we strategically position our organization to be successful in the future. The under-30 generation all want to talk about ethics and ethical practices and behavior and the role of governance to achieve it. They want to understand not just ethical behavior but how the organization got there."

Julie felt that the range of topics and the case studies gave her a different view of her work and would help further develop her leadership competencies. One small issue: She wished they had more time to work on the case studies so that discussion from the different perspectives could be richer and more fully understood.

Julie's organization, driven by changes in its leadership and the changing environment of organizational behavior, has been going through many culture changes, and this course fitted perfectly with the new direction, so Julie found the course to be really good and also gave her approaches that she could actively follow up in her job. Based on her background, she believes that the focus on ethical behaviors applies in all sectors, especially with younger groups:

"If you don't have ethical behaviors, then your culture is toxic and you will lose good people with all the costs of turnover and replacement."

The research about ethics and compliance and the impact on the reputation of organizations, supports Julie's observation.

Julie will encourage her team and colleagues to take the program but believes the learning should be built into all leadership and management programs and especially those dealing with equity, diversity and inclusion. ("EDI") Julie was surprised that such courses did not have content on ethics:

"If you are going to talk about EDI in your organization, how can you not talk about ethical behaviors and compliance? And compliance is not just from a legal perspective!"

Cases and Viewpoints #6.2: A look at reputation and compliance issues in advertising and marketing with Gowling WLG.

A multinational law firm headquartered in Ottawa, it was formed by the combination of Canada-based Gowlings, originally founded in 1887, and UK-based Wragge Lawrence Graham & Co in 2016. In Canada Gowlings has 1,500 lawyers in 19 offices.

Interview with Brenda Pritchard, Partner and Daniel Cole, Department Head Toronto IP Group.

Starting as an early specialist in marketing communication before it became a specialist area, Brenda's almost four-decade career with Gowling led her to become the preeminent legal authority in the discipline. Daniel Cole joined to work with Brenda in 2006. They are co-authors of the book *Advertising and Marketing Law in Canada*. Together with a team of talented advertising lawyers, they built a major practice area serving the marketing and particularly the marketing communications sector. While they were in growth mode before the digital age, the expansion since has been dramatic. As Brenda described the evolution: *"This new social media moved us all from "boob tube" to YouTube."*

Advertising Claims

The move from checking advertising claims before use in traditional media is now much more complex. First, in speed of communication. As Daniel commented:

"When I started, messages in traditional media were carefully crafted and legally cleared. Now the speed with which messages go out in social media means that there is very little if any legal oversight."

Second, so much online communication is conversational:

"It's like having conversations with your closest friends. If you don't appeal to them in your messaging, you will hear about it!"

Third, in this conversational environment, mistakes and misleading statements often lead to problems, so a lot of work is done correcting misstatements:

"Cleaning it up! A lot of times it is not so much a legal risk as a reputational risk."

These three areas have made brand management and brand communication issues:

"Harder and more challenging."

This is particularly true of live events where however much spokespeople are alerted to risks of misstatement or false statements, there will often have to be extensive follow up to protect the brand. Now, influencers are now subject to quite strict rules on what they can say and cannot say.

Additionally, if there has been "a big lie" from a competitor or someone that hurts your brand, the task is to find ways to correct it, especially if there are product liability issues involved.

Unlike the US, which often has increasingly stringent legislation, in Canada issues like revealing the influencer's employer is often handled by a voluntary code. The Canadian Code of Advertising Standards has a focus on "Truth. Fairness. Accuracy." The Code contains 14 provisions that set the criteria for advertising that is truthful, fair and accurate; these are regularly updated. The Council now provides an "Ad Standards Clearance Check Mark" for claims that it has reviewed and cleared.

Sometimes a more legislative approach is used and the Competition Bureau Canada is brought in. The Competition Bureau is an independent law enforcement agency under the Competition Act whose mission is to protect and promote competition for the benefit of Canadian consumers and businesses. Its mandate is to review deceptive marketing practices; labelling; frauds and scams, bid-rigging, price fixing and illegal agreements, mergers and acquisitions, and restrictive trade practices. Their work does include misleading advertising issues.

In Daniel's view, sometimes the Competition Bureau may appear slow in responding to changes in US law, practice or social media movements. Part of the reason is, as Daniel comments: *"Because they have broad general rules prohibiting misleading advertising, they sometimes take the view that these rules already address the concerns in social media too. Sometimes they do, but sometimes their application is not straightforward."*

Privacy

In addition, the European Union privacy regulations are being stepped up. As Daniel comments:

"In Canada we now have multiple pieces of privacy legislation coming in, in the next little while. I do think we trail, but it is such a hot button issue—the currency of data—that legislation can't lag too far behind. I do expect to see pretty quick movement on trying to get it right from a privacy perspective."

Compliance

As far as compliance issues are concerned, as Brenda points out all or most large organizations do have policies:

"Policies where your job depends on following them. Legal counsel is usually in charge of compliance follow up to ensure standards are followed—for instance, technical standards that must be fully substantiated."

Small- and medium-sized enterprises (SMEs) may be less complete in compliance policies and processes, but when legal counsel is brought in, Daniel indicates:

"We've written lots of guidelines about what employees can do when representing the company: what disclosures can or must they make. We have clients who have significant moderation policies from a social media perspective. If something happens, how does it get escalated, how does it get dealt with? We draft 'playbooks' and create guidelines indicating that if you are playing in this 'sandbox' here's what to watch out for. Typically, not every single social media statement can be examined due to the speed of this media."

The issue is often that while there may be policies, these may not be adequately communicated to all employees in playbooks of how to action the policies given the speed of movement in social media. As Brenda says, *"The key is to have the legal team working across operational departments and ensuring appropriate communication and training."*

Beyond Compliance to Integrity

Increasingly the issue is not just compliance but reputation and that requires a greater focus on integrity. Now, as both Brenda and Daniel say, *"Legal advice is not just about the exact claim or statement in a public communication, but the general impression."*

Brenda goes on, that in contemporary marketing communication it is not just the words and pictures but the impression:

"Everything put together, what do I think they [the audience] *heard and saw."*

Daniel adds:

"We are now brand protectors."

Future Issues

The issues for the future are complex and will require legal advisors to work closely with other senior organization and government groups to construct effective policies and practices. Examples of issues emerging are:

- AI and with it issues of credibility, communication clarity and copyright;

- Augmented and virtual reality manipulations to create a superior general impression that is not the in-reality experience;

- How to legitimately "convince people to consume content" (Daniel) as they don't want to be advertised to;

- How to handle the increasingly difficult issues around pricing: dynamic pricing, drip pricing, the regular versus discounted price, and so on.

- How to strike the balance between admission of ethical and/or compliance error and just fixing the problem.

And the big issue for the future with customers, employees, suppliers, investors and legislators is privacy. How far do we collect and use data from various sources—even with some permission—to impact purchase decisions?

"It is the interplay between the legal review, the strict legal review, the brand and reputational considerations and issues of ethics and integrity."

Daniel

"It's what do I think I just communicated, and can I support that?"

Brenda

Interview: March 10, 2023.

CHAPTER 7

REPUTATION MANAGEMENT THROUGH ETHICS, COMPLIANCE, BRANDING, AND PUBLIC RELATIONS

"I would rather go to any extreme than suffer anything that is unworthy of my reputation or that of my crown."

– Elizabeth I., 1533–1602, English, Queen of England 1558–1602

"Glass, China, and reputation are easily cracked and never well mended."

– Benjamin Franklin, 1706–1790, American inventor, philosopher and statesman

In this world of constant information, viewpoints, and rumour it is hard to manage organizational reputation. It is especially hard when the target groups are so extensive: investors, Board, current and potential staff, current and potential customers, suppliers, influencers, media, government, and not-for-profits.

Building a strong reputation comes down to leadership followed up by a strong organization culture that sees ethical behaviours and practices as essential elements in performance. Many authors and researchers see this values-based leadership as essential for organizations to thrive. Mark Carney in his book *Value(s)* discusses the characteristics of values-based leadership:

"There are five essential and universal attributes of leadership:

1. Purpose

2. Perspective

3. Clarity

4. Competence

5. Humility."

His book is a powerful argument for each of these. He states the case for a strong values-based approach to replace an over-emphasis on narrow, short-term profit-maximising approaches. This is a necessary ingredient to build a sustainable, positive reputation.

As indicated throughout this book, it is important that each organization is clear about its values (as indicated in the Reputation Management Strategy Hierarchy Tool – Intro. on page 18) and then through policy and then detailed communication and training (as indicated in in the Reputation Management Strategy Action Plan in Chapter 6) its ability to build these values and policies into regular practice. It is also important that these are incorporated into strategy and material of at least two key marketing activities:

- Brand Plan

- PR in the Marketing Communications Plan

Brand Plan

Whether the brand is the corporate name or product/service—specific brands under the corporate umbrella—the inclusion of ethical and compliance standards must be actively considered.

Regarding my earlier definition of what a brand is: "A promise of benefits from a trusted source consistently delivered with the highest level of satisfaction versus direct and indirect competitors," it is important to note that in order to build reputational trust in the brand's "benefits" and "level of satisfaction," due attention must be paid to both the organization's ethical and compliance principles and specific challenges in the areas of data management, customer service, and customer pricing. There are many brand planning formats. One I have used in both practice and teaching is below with a suggested adaptation to guide attention to the challenges.

A modified Brand Planning Format (modifications indicated in bold type):

External Conditions:

1. Competitive Environment: Description of the marketplace and alternative choices as seen by the consumer/customer, and the relative value the brand offers.

2. Target: The person/organization and the situation for which the brand is the best choice. Defined in terms of their attitudes and values, not just demographics.

3. Insight: The element that all of you know about the target group and their needs upon which the brand is founded and developed.

Consumer/Customer Appeal:

1. Benefits: The differentiating functional and emotional benefits that motivate purchase and repurchase.

2. **Values: What the brand stands for and believes in.**

3. Personality: The personality characteristics that the brand should evoke.

4. Reason to Believe: The proof offered to substantiate the positioning.

5. Discriminator: The single most compelling and comprehensive statement the target group would make for buying and repurchasing the brand.

6. **Trust: What does the consumer/customer trust most about the brand: what issues of lower trust are there? How important to them?**

7. Essence: The distillation of the brand's genetic code into one clear thought.

As indicated in much brand literature (including my co-authored book *Ikonica*), brand planning in the modern era must be done within the context of "the 3 x Cs": commerce, culture, and community. This is especially true given the rise in importance of ethics and compliance issues and the trend towards more corporate branding with its heightened reputational risks.

Let's look at this ever-evolving context of branding:

Commerce: The commercial environment that sets both product/ service performance expectations and to some extent, socio-emotional expectations (e.g., status symbols).

Culture: The need for brand management to keep pace with evolving cultural and social mores. This will include issues of diversity, equity, and inclusion; labour demand and its impact on job status and remuneration; and climate and conservation issues. Here the internal cultural health is an important factor to avoid the toxicity that is so reputationally damaging.

Community: The need for brands to build strong community connections (physically and virtually) to gain positive, and avoid negative, reputational capital. As will be seen in the next PR section, this is behind much corporate philanthropy and engagement.

It is in the context of these changes that the brand plan must be developed and evaluated with regular tracking. In addition, the marketing communications delivery of brand reputation must include the same ethics and compliance questions.

PR in the Marketing Communications Plan

Concerns about organization and brand reputation should be a factor in planning and execution of all marketing communications: advertising in traditional media (TV, radio, magazine, newspaper and outdoor), social media networks (Facebook, YouTube, WhatsApp, Messenger, Instagram, WeChat, TikTok, Twitter, etc.); public relations (PR); and sales and consumer promotion.

All areas require ethical and compliance attention. In advertising for most traditional media categories there are regulations and pre-clearance compliance authorities. Many of these come under the federal Competition Act and its activities like Competition Bureau Enforcement Guidelines and the Deceptive Marketing Practices Directorate. The Competition Bureau Canada *"…is an independent law enforcement agency that protects and promotes competition for the benefit of Canadian consumers and businesses."*

The Bureau handles deceptive marketing practices, labelling, fraud and scams, bid-rigging, price fixing and illegal agreements, mergers and acquisitions, restrictive trade practices as well as cases of misleading advertisings.

The advertising industry also has a body that reviews cases. Established in 1963, The Canadian Code of Advertising Standards has a code that includes 14 provisions that set the criteria for acceptable advertising that is:

"Truthful. Fair and Accurate."

On cases assigned to it and passed, it now awards "The Clearance Services Check Mark" for use by the advertiser.

Internet-based social media has far less regulation and the ability for false or misleading promotion is much greater. Most "standards" have been set by social media/search engine organization owners like Google, but they are weak, unenforced, and in many cases controversial. This issue is likely to become ever more important as AI generated supplements like OpenAI's ChatGPT and Bing add automatically generated advice to search and the analytics sold to advertisers as a result.

In Canada as part of the Competition Act, the Competition Bureau Enforcement Guidelines through its "Application of the Competition Act to representation on the Internet," do keep a watch on social media communication. Attempts to legislate further, like Canada's Bill C-18 get caught up in the cross over issues of free speech and advertising. This is a classic area where ethical issues need to be clearly developed as compliance issues are often slow and incomplete. (Cases and Viewpoints #6.2 gives a legal firm's view on these issues).

In this chapter the focus is on PR. The reason for this lies in the importance of PR in reputation building through its activities:

- Crisis PR: handling negative publicity based on the kind of reputational crises discussed earlier in this book. Examples include Tide Pods that had teenagers eating them; Southwest Airlines and its first in-flight fatality; Starbucks and some racism issues.

- Cause-related PR: associating organizations with charitable, cause or other not-for-profit related organizations to the benefit of the funding organizations. Corporate donations in Canada amount to around $3 billion/year. Examples include Bell Canada and "Let's Talk" for funding mental illness work; Indigo and its "Love of Reading" fund; Loblaws and its "President's Choice Children's Charity Foundation"; BMO and its foodbank contributions.

- Lobbying: usually to influence legislators but now tied closely to social media use and the importance of the "influencers" on-line.

- Organization announcements: the stream of press releases, conferences and activities that highlight the announcements and activities regarding the organization.

The work is handled by both external agencies like Argyle, Edelman, and H&K, and internal departments. Due to the rise in importance of social media networks, its activity is growing in importance. Now a $1 billion activity in Canada, PR activities are now central to helping organizations manage their reputation. As such, adherence to the values of the organization as expressed through its ethics and compliance policies and practices, and its Brand Plan, are essential to avoid lapses in communications veracity and relevance, and enhance the positive aspects of its reputation. The Cases and Viewpoints #7.1 from Argyle PR that follows give insight into this arena.

Cases and Viewpoints 7.1: A look at Public Relations in Reputation Management with Riannon John from Argyle Integrated Public Relations Agency.

Argyle is a leading Canadian Public Relations Agency. It was formed in 1979 and from 2022 became part of the Believeco Partners integrated marketing group. With staff of 140, Argyle has offices in seven cities across Canada and the US. With clients like McDonald's, Hostess Brands, and the Organic Trade Association, Argyle provides advisors in Corporate Reputation and Communication Strategy, Public Stakeholder and Employee Engagement, and six other areas.

Riannon John, Vice President Sustainable Value, is an experienced communications and public relations executive with 15 years of experience working with World Wildlife Fund Canada, Mount Sinai Hospital in Toronto, Edelman, and Toronto Metropolitan University before joining Argyle.

As Riannon attests, the role and activity of public relations (PR) has changed considerably over the last two decades. It was always an important part of reputation management but has evolved substantially to meet the needs of client organizations. At the heart of this change is the digital world.

In June of 2007 Apple's iPhone was launched and the next years saw the rise of constant digital communication, social media, influencer importance, and more recently AI-enabled communication and analysis.

"The biggest fundamental change has been digital. In the early days digital was optional, now it is not. It has opened up whole new worlds for most organizations to tell their story."

As Riannon points out, traditional media coverage is still important in PR but now *"There are now so many tools in the PR toolbox."*

The digital world has also made a profound change in how organizations and their reputations are seen. Riannon quotes David Mattin from his February 2017 *Medium* article, "Our brand was a black box. Now it's a glass box":

Back in the day a business was a black box. For outsiders it was pretty hard to see what was going on inside. The brand was painted on the outside of the box. People came and looked at it. They either liked it or they didn't. Today a business is a glass box. Outsiders can easily see inside. They can see the people and the processes. They can see the values. They can even see what the people inside the box feel about what they are doing."

This higher level of transparency in organizational activities has led to a greater focus on authenticity in communication.

"There is less acceptance of organizations saying one thing and doing another, even though it still happens with issues like greenwashing and so on."

The key in managing reputation is to

"Act in good faith and to be clear and consistent and, as the kids say today, 'provide receipts.' You can't just make claims. You have to back them up with evidence: proof of action."

While crisis management is still a major activity for PR agencies, there is now more focus on risk mitigation recommendations that incorporate codes of ethics and/or compliance that seek to avoid the reputational crises.

"Today, we advise our clients on both what we can do to protect them and also what they should change."

The nature of the issue and its degree of seriousness determines the management level involved and how much response is directed externally or internally. One clear trend though is that there is more overall focus at all levels, though Riannon feels that internal employee communication briefing and training does need to improve further.

"I always advocate for informing employees as the first audience, if not the primary audience. They are the ones that will have to answer the questions in almost any scenario. Without proper communication and briefing, they may unintentionally give the wrong information and unwittingly perpetuate the issue."

In determining any PR strategy, the key is to be clear about who is the target group. The explosion of digital media has made this essential.

"'All Canadians' is not an acceptable answer. I like to be really, really targeted and to know as much about those audiences as I can. To cut through the noise and clutter of the digital world, we need to say the right thing, to the right people, in the right way, at the right time and in the right place."

An example would be to reach Gen Z where Facebook would not be the right vehicle, as I discovered constantly in my own teaching of undergraduates. For this group it could be TikTok, Triller, Snapchat, Byte or other video sharing, and to then use a respected influencer. In consumer goods particularly, well-chosen influencers are increasingly important. Along with other target groups, experts, scientists, academics, or recognized thought leaders also have a strong influence on issues and/or product and service selection. Many PR organizations now have their own rating and evaluation systems to evaluate influencer fit and credibility to particular target groups. In some countries like the US there are now regulations that direct influencers to declare what organizations are paying them for their comments. Repetition of message is key as well as the way the message is conveyed:

"The key is to be audience-centric in your approach. Too often we fall into the trap of 'This is what we want the audience to know' rather than how do we give the information to them in a way that will make them open to receiving it and in a way that adds value for them."

A big ongoing challenge for the PR industry is the evaluation of its effectiveness. Measurement of number of media stories still exists but is less relevant. However, the 2023 Edelman Trust Barometer still indicates that in Canada traditional media is still the most trusted.

Attempts at higher value metrics like measures of engagement and assessment of perception about a brand's reputation or an issue are growing. In addition, analytics can assist in tracking what led target groups to a website and how they followed up; website "heat maps" tend to be well used. While many senior executives want hard numbers for return on PR investment in reputation management, this linear relationship is not always fathomable. However, as Riannon points out,

"There is value in combining qualitative and quantitative metrics to assess the impact of communications efforts to build or manage reputations. There's just no single metric that captures all of this, nor is there the same ability to track journeys that we see in digital marketing."

Failure to address reputationally damaging issues by not addressing them financially or operationally often prove most costly.

"If you ignore these things, they just compound!"

This is beginning to be better understood. What has changed here is a greater general understanding of the value of the brand and the importance of a positive reputation. Surveys like Argyle's "Public Relationships Index," Edelman's "Trust Barometer," and Leger's "Reputation Study" are examples.

Brand reputation management issues have given rise to a number of newer trends:

- Growth of what is termed as brand journalism: "telling your own story."

- Growth of sponsored activities with reputable parties like the not-for-profit sector and events held for "good causes" by the organization itself. Examples include Canadian Tire and the "Jumpstart" kids' program, Indigo and the "Love of Reading Fund," Loblaw and the "Presidents Choice Charity Foundation," Mountain Equipment Co-op, and wilderness conservation.

"Probably one of the most powerful reputational strategies."

- Greater cross over between internal employee communication and external. Today we should assume that all internal communication will be shared externally.

- More organizations are looking for guidance on how to navigate changing social norms and social issues. For example, how to respond to movements like "Black Lives Matter" and Indigenous Peoples issues: *"There is a lot of fear around doing something wrong in these spaces, but there are opportunities—and expectations—for organizations to step up."*

- A move towards integration in marketing communication between advertising and PR, as an example, agencies like Believeco Partners and Wunderman Thompson.

- Also, more integration across all organizational disciplines/silos to build stronger culture: *"Your reputation hangs in the balance in everything you do."*

Other issues that are prompting greater attention in the PR sector include data mismanagement and illegal or misleading financial statements and information. In addition, there is the issue of the mental and physical state of the workplace for employees and the effect this has on customer satisfaction and most importantly, the overall organization culture. Riannon believes HR departments need to become more involved in the strategic issues and policies that lead to improving organizational culture. She believes this is particularly true of employee communications:

"There is room for improvement in many organizations for employee communications including around launches of new services and products, new platforms, new policies and practices, or any large organizational change. This is especially true when you talk about issues of compliance. This requires direct communication and training but is also a cultural issue. The best way to ensure compliance is to have developed a culture that supports it and even celebrates it. This area does not receive enough attention."

There is need, in her view, to combine the knowledge and skill sets of legal and compliance with HR and employee work and communications.

In terms of general ethical behaviour, Argyle does itself have a set of policies and these include data security and privacy, defining some organizations, and activities with which they will not engage. This is shared as part of onboarding and ongoing communication as well as discussion when particular client issues arise. These types of policies are increasingly important for all organizations:

"This part of culture is not just a 'nice to have.' It really is a risk mitigation strategy and reputation protection strategy, albeit hard to measure, hard to mandate and often dependent on great leadership. We need to think about reputation as something that touches every part of the organization

*and as communicators our role is to draw these pieces together: to be more
progressive, be more forward thinking, be more ethical."*

Interview March 9, 2023.

Cases and Viewpoints #7.2:
Maple Leaf Foods

**A famous Canadian case that Maple Leaf Foods experienced in 2008
shows not only the reputational risk vulnerability but evidence of
how good management response and practice has positive impact
on reputation and business.**

Back in 2007 Maple leaf Foods was a successful food processing
company of $5.2 billion revenue, earnings of $199 million, selling
packaged, fresh, and frozen meat and bakery products and an
agribusiness operation under brands such as "Maple Leaf," "Schneiders,"
"Dempster's" and others, in Canada, the UK, and the US. Michael H.
McCain was President/CEO and a major shareholder with about one
third of the equity following his acquisition of the company with the
backing of the Ontario Teachers' Pension Fund in 1995.

The plants preparing deli meats met both Canadian and US health
standards, but in summer 2008 an outbreak of Listeriosis was detected
at the Barton Road Toronto facility. The infection was caused by the
bacterium *Listeria monocytogenes*, which infected a line of, initially, 23
ready-to-eat packaged meats, and then up to 220 deli meats, probably
from accumulation of bacteria on its meat-slicing equipment. On
August 17, before the Canadian Food Inspection Agency ordered it,
Maple Leaf issued a voluntary recall. From then to early September
the recall and facility closure was extended. However, during this
time the tragic death toll mounted especially amongst the elderly with
compromised immune systems. Deaths mounted to 22 with others
suffering multiple serious symptoms.

The serious situation led to the closing of the Barton Road facility
for months while the facility was extensively cleaned and much of

the machinery replaced. Not surprisingly the media coverage and investigations by the Public Health Agency of Canada (PHAC) and the Canadian Food Inspection Agency (CFIA) had an immediate effect on Maple Leaf brand sales, which initially shrank by 35%.

Michael McCain brought in Linda Smith an experienced PR executive to aid him with the issue/crisis management strategy. Linda's substantial experience with Hill & Knowlton, then as founder of Fleishman-Hillard in Canada, aided the thinking and the actions.

Against the advice of his legal and financial advisers, Michael McCain went on TV and in other media describing and admitting the problem and outlining what was being done to ensure the problem was not repeated. On August 28, he issued this apology and statement:

"My name is Michael McCain. As you may know Listeria was found in some of our products. Even though Listeria is a bacteria commonly found in many foods and in the environment, we work diligently to eliminate it. When Listeria was discovered in the product we launched immediate recalls to get it off the shelf. Then we shut the plant down. Tragically our products have been linked to illnesses and loss of life. To Canadians who are ill and to the families who have lost loved ones I offer my deepest sympathies. Words cannot begin to express our sadness for your pain. Maple Leaf Foods is 23,000 people who live in a culture of food safety. We have an unwavering commitment to keeping your food safe with standards well beyond regulatory requirements. But this week our best efforts failed and we are deeply sorry. This is the toughest situation we've faced in 100 years as a company. We know that this has shaken your confidence in us. I commit to you that our actions are guided by putting your interest first."

Criticism in the media reduced. By a couple of months later, sales had recovered somewhat and were only down 15%. Michael McCain commented:

"We felt that [the apology] was the responsible thing to do at the time and we knew it would have a very substantial financial consequence… our belief is that over time by behaving responsibly, we will be respected and possibly rewarded by our customers."

Financial results from the meat division that year were predictably poor: recall costs for the year were $37.5 million and lawsuits eventually cost another $25 million. However, by the following fiscal year (2009) the meat products division revenue had recovered to $55.4 million from the $29.5 million in fiscal 2008 with its third and fourth quarter impact of the *Listeria* recall. Additionally, by 2022 the year Michael McCain stepped down as President/CEO the Maple Leaf brand is 21st of brands with a positive reputation (see Leger Research in Case #3).

Arguments still continue about Maple Leaf Foods responsibility for the crisis and the response. However, there is no doubt that the openness of Michael McCain's action resulted in successful continuation of the Maple Leaf meat brand and its financial viability.

CHAPTER 8
SUMMARY

"A good reputation is more valuable than money."

– Publilius Syrus, 1ˢᵗ century BC, Roman writer of aphorisms

"When the world is silent even one voice is powerful."

– Malala Yousafzai, Nobel Peace Prize winner.

We work in a society demonstrating increasing concern and respect for practices exhibiting appropriate respect for diversity, equity and inclusion, conservation, respectful treatment of staff, customers, suppliers, partners, investors, and, the local, national and international community. Organizational decisions about its financial returns must be made in this context. Organization reputation develops in this context. Although in monopolistic or oligopolistic markets bad organization behaviour may continue and organizations with poor reputations may survive, the evidence is that a reputation for appropriate ethical, compliant, and business practices with appropriate values, will have both moral and financial rewards.

To build and sustain a positive reputation and avoid a negative one requires the attention, policies, procedures, practices and communication outlined in this book. To summarise we will follow the "5 x Ws" format to outline what organizations and their marketing groups should do.

What

What are our organization's values? How do these fit with our organization's vision, mission and goals? How do they fit in with contemporary good ethical and compliance practice? How do these transfer into appropriately ethical and compliant behaviour by all members of our organization? What costs do these incur and what do we do to properly fund them?

Why

Why is this important? All Board and organization personnel need to be clear about the positive advantages of appropriate behaviour, and the risks from inappropriate unethical, non-compliant behaviour.

Who

Who develops these policies, procedures, and practices? The answer is engagement by representatives of all departments and levels. Who should be briefed and trained in these procedures and practices? Answer: everyone employed in, or connected with, the organization.

Where

Where should staff briefing and training take place? In the local work environment of staff. The briefing and training should be included in regular workplace briefings and meetings: they must become part of the "DNA" of the culture. Where should external briefing take place and responses made to negatives about the organizations policy, procedures and practices? Communication content and delivery must reflect the core values and policies and use the media and mode best suited to the organization's culture and target group.

When

When should these policies, procedures, and practices be implemented and briefed? As soon as they are developed and briefing and training actioned. These should be reviewed regularly with updates based on socio-cultural and legal changes.

Cases and Viewpoints #8.1: O Canada.

There are many surveys globally that look at different aspects of national achievement, To conclude this book on reputation let's look Canada's reputation based on 20 of these. For comparison France, the UK, and the US will be shown.

1. **Socio-Economic**

Deloitte Social Progress Index 2022: Canada is 10th out of 130 countries; UK is 19th, France is 20th, US is 25th.

Three outcome dimensions with 12 components: Basic Human Needs, Foundations of Wellbeing (access to knowledge, eco-sustainability etc.), Opportunity (personal rights, equity etc.)

Edelman Trust Barometer 2023: Canada scored 52 out of 100: a Neutral ranking US ranked Low Trust at 48 as did UK at 43

Survey of 32,000 respondents (1,500/country) in 28 countries that measure trust in government and social institutions.

EIU Environmental, Social and Governance (ESG) Risk 2023: Canada overall ranked "Very low risk" as did France and UK, US ranked "Low risk." Components:

Country	Environment	Social	Governance
Canada	Moderate	Very low	Very low
France	Very low	Low	Very low
UK	Very low	Very low	Very low
US	Moderate	Very low	Very low

Ninety components covering how governments, society and businesses impact a country's sustainability.

EIU Democracy Index 2022: Canada ranked 12th out of 168 countries, UK is 18th, France is 22nd, US is 30th.

Sixty measures of electoral process and pluralism, functioning of government, political participation, political culture, civil liberties.

Heritage Institute Index of Economic Freedom 2023: Canada ranked 16th out of 180 countries; US is 25th, UK is 28th, France is 51st.

Composite measures of 12 freedoms: rule of law, government size, regulatory efficiency, open markets, free competition, strong legal protection for property, etc.

IMD World Competitiveness Ranking 2022: Canada ranked 14th out of 56 countries; US is 10th, UK is 23rd, France is 28th.

Three hundred and thirty-three competitiveness criteria for economic performance, government efficiency, business efficiency, infrastructure.

INSEAD Global Innovation Index 2022: Canada ranked 15th out of 130 countries; US ranked 2nd, UK ranked 4th, France ranked 12th.

Measures include infrastructure, human capital, market sophistication, knowledge & technical outputs, creative outputs etc.

Legatum Prosperity Index 2023: Canada is 13th out of 170 countries; UK is 12th, US is 19th, France is 23rd.

A composite of measures for economy, entrepreneurship & opportunity, governance, education, health, safety & security, personal freedom, social capital, natural environment.

OECD Better Life Index 2023: Canada is 10th out of 37 countries; US is 8th, UK is 15th, France is 18th.

Eleven criteria including housing, education, health, income, jobs, civic engagement, community, environment, safety, work-life balance, life satisfaction.

OECD Progress for International Assessment of Adult Competencies (PIAAC) 2016/17: 24

Country	Literacy	Numeracy
Canada	273.5	265.5
UK	272.5	261.7
US	269.5	252.8
France	262.1	254.3

Five thousand respondents /country tested.

Reporters Without Borders

World Press Freedom In2023

Canada ranked 15th out of 180 countries; France is 24th, UK is 26th, US is 45th

Journalist's assessments of pluralism, independence, transparency, legislative abuses, infrastructure.

Transparency International Corruption Perceptions Index 2022: high ranking is low corruption: Canada is 13th out of 158; UK is 11th, France is 22nd, US is 27th.

Criteria are the perception of corruption at all society levels

UN Human Development Index 2022:

Canada is 15th out of 191 countries; UK is 18th, US is 21st, France is 28th.

Multiple measures based on three overall criteria: healthy life, knowledge, standard of living.

UN World Happiness Index 2023:

Canada is 14th out of 155 countries; UK is 17th, US is 19th, France is 21st.

1,000 criteria including GDP/capita, social support, healthy life expectancy, freedom of life choices, generosity etc.

World Bank GINI Index 2021:

190 countries; 0= everyone has the same income: Canada is 33.3, France 32.4, UK 35.1, US 41.5.

Poverty and inequality data from household surveys and government records.

2. **National Brand Reputation Strength**

Brand Finance – National Brand Value 2023:

Canada was 8th out of 81 countries valued at brand value of US\$2,621 billion; US was #1 at \$30,301b, UK was #4 at \$4,797b, France was #6 at \$3,676b.

Bloom Consulting Country Brand Ranking 2022/2023 Trade Edition:

Canada ranked 10th out of 206 countries; UK was 1st, US was 2nd, France was 4th.

A proprietary algorithm assembling economic performance, digital demand, current brand strategy, and online performance.

Future Brand Country Brand Index 2020:

Canada ranked 5th out of 75 countries; US was 13th, France was 14th, US was 20th.

Brand perception dimensions: awareness, familiarity, associations, preference, visitation etc.

Institute for Economics and Peace Global Peace Index 2023: Canada ranked 12th out of 165 countries, UK is 34th, France is 65th, US is 129th.

25 indicators of both domestic and international conflict, society safety and security, degree of militarization.

US News & World Report/ BAV Consulting/ Wharton, World's Best Countries 2022: Canada ranked 3rd out of 80 countries; US was 4th, UK was 8th, France was 19th.

Sixty-five factors including adventure, citizenship, economic influence, entrepreneurship, heritage, quality of life, etc.

"Now this is not the end. It is not even the beginning of the end. But it is, perhaps, the end of the beginning."

– Winston Churchill

BIBLIOGRAPHY

"Reputation. Reputation. Reputation. Oh, I have lost my reputation. I have lost the immortal part of myself and what remains is bestial."

– Cassio in Act 2, Scene 3 in *Othello* by William Shakespeare

Bazerman, Max and Tenbrunsel, Ann E. *Blind Spots – Why We Fail to Do What's Right and What to Do About It*, Princeton University Press 2012.

Boatright, John R. *Ethics in Finance – 3rd Edition*, Wiley Blackwell, 2014.

Carmichael, D. Soonawalla, K. and Stroehle, J. "Sustainability Assurance as Greenwashing" *Stanford Social Innovation Review*, Winter 2023 pp 35–39.

Carney, Mark. *Value(s) – Building a Better World for All*, Signal McClelland Stewart, 2021.

CBC TV "Marketplace": "What the Fee" broadcast, February 10, 2023.

CPA Ontario "Ethics in Practice" Seminar, December 8, 2022. Speakers:

- Janet Gilles, Executive Vice -President Regulatory & Standards, CPA

- Morgan Hamel, *President MH Partners*

- Lisa Dorion, *Corporate ethics, compliance and risk management consultant*

- Prof. Krista Fiolleau PhD, *University of Waterloo.*

- Prof. Robert Steinbauer PhD, *Brock University*

- Prof. Kelly Richmond Pope PhD, *De Paul University, Chicago, USA*

Edelman Trust Barometer, 2023.

ESG Global Advisors and Argyle. "The State of Social in ESG," November 2022.

Ethics & Compliance Initiative (ECI) www.ethics.org

Ethisphere: www.worldsmostethicalcompanies.com

Grunig, James E. *Excellence in Public Relations and Communications Management*, Routledge, 1992.

Guzman, Monica. *I Never Thought of it That Way: How to Have Fearlessly Curious Conversations in Dangerously Divided Times*, BenBella Books 2022.

HEC University of Montreal "Certification in Ethics & Compliance" course, 2022.

Hamel, Gary + Zanina, Michele *Humanocracy – Creating Organizations as Amazing as the People Inside Them*, Harvard Business Review Press, 2020.

Hamel, Morgan and Davey, Keith. "A New Era of Stakeholder Activism: why we are disoriented and what to do about it." Online essay 2022.

Helpscout.ca "107 Customer Service Statistics and Facts You Shouldn't Ignore," November 22, 2022.

Kahneman, Daniel. *Thinking Fast and Slow*, Farrar, Straus & Giroux, 2011.

Kincaide, David. *The Brand-Driven CEO – Embedding Brand into Business Strategy*, University of Toronto Press, 2020.

Leger: 2023 Reputation Study.

Macdonald, William A. *Might Nature Be Canadian? – Essays on Mutual Accommodation* McGill-Queens University Press, 2020.

McKinsey & Company Risk & Resilience: "The EU Digital Strategy: The impact of data privacy on global business." March 1, 2023 Commentary.

McKinsey Global Institute: "Performance through People – Transforming human capital into competitive advantage," February 2, 2023 update.

McKinsey Company Impact Study: "How a New Zealand retailer reinvented itself around customer satisfaction," January 31, 2023.

Romaniuk, Jenni and Sharp, Byron *"How Brands Grow – Part 2"* Oxford University Press 2022

Sandel, Michael J. *Justice – What's the Right Thing to Do?*, Farrar, Straus and Giroux, 2009.

Schreiber, Elliot S. *The Yin & Yang of Reputation Management*, Enlightened Enterprise Media, 2021.

Society of Corporate Compliance and Ethics: www.corporatecompliance.org

The Economist:

- February 25, 2023: "Scientific Fraud - Doctored Data," pages 79–82

- "The World Ahead 2023" edition: "Time to take a stand," page 118.

- -November 12, 2022: "A guide to corporate fraud" pages 57, 58.

The Markup.org/privacy/2023 "Forget Milk and Eggs: Supermarkets are Having a Fire Sale on Data about You." February 16, 2023.

Trace International: www.traceinternational.org

Tucker, K. Perry, R.L. Singleton, P. *Marketing Guides – Reputation Management*, Ducttape Publishing, 2017

Veliz, Carissa. *Privacy is Power – Why and How You Should Take Back Control of Your Data* Corgi Books, 2020.

ABOUT THE AUTHOR

"We know what we are, but know not what we may become."

– Ophelia from *Hamlet*, Act 4, Scene 5. – William Shakespeare

His 25-year practitioner career includes marketing roles with the Universal Oil Products Company (UOP Inc.) in Chicago, USA; Esso Petroleum in Oslo, Norway, an entrepreneurial stint with Amca Marketing Inc. in Toronto and a career in advertising with the J. Walter Thompson (JWT) advertising agency in the UK, Canada and Japan concluding as President/CEO of JWT Japan and Executive Vice President and a Board Director of the worldwide company.

His 26-year academic career includes teaching at the Rutgers Graduate School of Business in the US, leading business schools in Argentina, China, India, Russia, and Thailand, and from 1998 - 2020 the marketing faculty at the Schulich School of Business, York University where he concluded as Distinguished Adjunct Professor of Marketing. From 2001-2020 he was also Executive Director of the Schulich Executive Education Centre (SEEC) which ran non-degree programs for over 10,000 executives and managers a year domestically and internationally. SEEC was continuously ranked in the top 45 executive and management training organizations in the world.

Alan co-authored the books *Advertising Works II*, and *Ikonica – A Field Guide to Canada's Brandscape* and has numerous papers and book chapters published. For AMA Toronto he authored *Mentorship Matters – Now More than Ever* published in 2021, and *Marketing Matters for Small & Medium Enterprises* in 2022.

He is an Associate Professor, HEC University of Montreal and works on their Executive Education group Ethics and Compliance programs. He teaches marketing and strategy for entrepreneurs at AMA Toronto, YEDI and others.

He sits on Not-For-Profit Boards and Board Committees. These include being a founding Advisory Board member of the AMA Toronto Mentor Exchange. He was voted on to the AMA Canadian Marketing Hall of Legends in the Mentor category in 2005.

He is a co-founder of the Cassie advertising awards, a holder of the ACA Gold Medal for contribution to the marketing industry, the Queen Elizabeth II Diamond Jubilee Medal for service to the literacy movement, and International Association of Business Communicators Toronto Communicator of the Year award.

www.ingramcontent.com/pod-product-compliance
Lightning Source LLC
Chambersburg PA
CBHW050954050726
47592CB00007B/2560